Critical Constructivism

PRIMER

PETER LANG
New York • Washington, D.C./Baltimore • Bern
Frankfurt am Main • Berlin • Brussels • Vienna • Oxford

Joe L. Kincheloe

Critical Constructivism
PRIMER

PETER LANG
New York • Washington, D.C./Baltimore • Bern
Frankfurt am Main • Berlin • Brussels • Vienna • Oxford

Library of Congress Cataloging-in-Publication Data

Kincheloe, Joe L..
Critical constructivism primer / Joe L. Kincheloe
p. cm.
Includes bibliographical references.
1. Constructivism (Education) 2. Critical pedagogy. I. Title.
LB1590.3.K53 370.11'5—dc22 2004030296
ISBN 0-8204-7616-1

Bibliographic information published by **Die Deutsche Bibliothek**.
Die Deutsche Bibliothek lists this publication in the "Deutsche Nationalbibliografie"; detailed bibliographic data is available on the Internet at http://dnb.ddb.de/.

Cover design by Lisa Barfield

The paper in this book meets the guidelines for permanence and durability of the Committee on Production Guidelines for Book Longevity of the Council of Library Resources.

275 Seventh Avenue, 28th Floor, New York, NY 10001
www.peterlangusa.com

Printed in the United States of America

Table of Contents

EDITOR'S NOTE

Twelve central points are made about critical constructivism in this primer; they are interspersed throughout the text. An explanation of each point follows its boldface exposition.

CHAPTER ONE

From Constructivism to Critical Constructivism

There has been a lot of talk and writing in the education profession over the last couple of decades about the nature of constructivism and its relationship to teaching and learning. Often when I listen to individuals talk about the concept, I discern much confusion and misunderstanding. In this context I offer this primer on constructivism and my particular "take" on it—critical constructivism. Throughout this volume I will provide clear descriptions and definitions of a variety of concepts related to critical constructivism and show you how they relate to the teaching and learning processes. At the same time I believe that education students and teachers are not sufficiently challenged in both their professional education and liberal arts and sciences classes, and in this context I will offer some complex ideas. The topic of constructivism is unalterably complex and cannot be made less so. The purpose of the book, however, is to maintain the integrity and complexity of the topic while introducing the reader to it in a smart and accessible manner. I hope you find my efforts helpful.

With these goals in mind the book presents several major concepts about critical constructivism. Each of these points is directly connected to the inseparable acts of teaching and knowledge production. Thus, critical constructivism is constantly concerned about research and pedagogy and the multiple ways they are connected. Over the next five chapters I will delineate these dimensions of critical constructivism one by one. Written in this manner, the book can be viewed as a whole or as separate parts to be read independently. The points fit together synergistically, as understanding one concept will enhance your understanding of the others. Writing the book in this manner is not designed to fragment the concept of critical constructivism but to give those new to the concept better access to its main dynamics.

Here are the main ideas of the book:

- The world is socially constructed—what we know about the world always involves a knower and that which is to be known. How the knower constructs the known constitutes what we think of as reality.
- All knowers are historical and social subjects. We all come from a "somewhere" which is located in a particular historical time frame. These spatial and temporal settings always shape the nature of our constructions of the world.
- Not only is the world socially and historically constructed, but so are people and the knowledge people possess. We create ourselves with the cultural tools at hand. We operate and construct the world and our lives on a particular social, cultural and historical playing field.
- A key aspect of education in this context involves understanding the nature of these constructions. In the realm of knowledge (the epistemological domain), it is simple-minded and misleading to merely study random outcomes of the construction process—isolated "facts" and

"truths." Constructivists are as much concerned with the processes through which certain information becomes validated knowledge as with committing lots of it to memory. They are also concerned with the processes through which certain information was not deemed to be worthy or validated knowledge.

- The teaching and learning process is intimately connected to the research act. Thus, throughout this book I will blur these categories and consistently examine knowledge production and research at the same time I am analyzing teaching and learning. A key dimension of critical constructivism involves the complex interrelationship between teaching and learning and knowledge production and research.
- When critical constructivists produce knowledge, they are not attempting to reduce variables but to maximize (Knoble, 1999) them. Such maximization produces a thicker, more detailed, more complex understanding of the social, political, economic, cultural, psychological and pedagogical world.
- Thus, the purpose of education in this critical constructivist process is not to transmit a body of validated truths to students for memorization. Instead, critical constructivists argue that a central role of schooling involves engaging students in the knowledge production process. A central dimension of teaching in this context involves engaging students in analyzing, interpreting and constructing a wide variety of knowledges emerging from diverse locations.
- Critical constructivists are concerned with the exaggerated role power plays in these construction and validation processes. Critical constructivists are particularly interested in the ways these processes help privilege some people and marginalize others.
- Critical constructivists reiterate the notion that knowledge is not a substance that can be deposited like money in a bank (Freire, 1970) and

taken out when time for its use arrives. In this transmissive theory of knowledge, information is transferred from the teacher to the pupil's mind. In the critical constructivist formulation, knowledge is constructed in the minds of human beings—minds that are constructed by the society around them (Tobin, 1993; Tobin and Tippins, 1993; Geeland, 1996).

- The knowledge of the classroom is constructed where students' personal experience intersects with academic knowledges. A key skill of a critical constructivist teacher involves nurturing this synthesis of personal experience and academic knowledge. Such a pedagogical act is extremely complex, and teachers must work hard to bring the different perspectives together. They reveal how their own perspectives came to be constructed and how the social values, ideologies and information they encounter shape their pedagogies and worldviews.
- In their search for ways to produce democratic and evocative knowledges, critical constructivists become detectives of new ways of seeing and constructing the world. In this context they come to value knowledges and forms of meaning-making traditionally dismissed by dominant culture and mainstream academics. In this subjugated context they use the African American blues idiom to construct "blue knowledge."

I believe that a rigorous and detailed understanding of these concepts will change education as we now know it to something far more compelling and useful. Such understanding will help us produce passionate and insightful scholars capable of changing the world for the better.

Introducing the Concept: What Are We Talking About?

The understanding of constructivism and critical constructivism helps us make sense of the educational world that surrounds us in a rigorous and thoughtful way. In the twenty-first century, the idea that teachers need to understand the complexity of the educational world is almost a radical proposition in and of itself—many educational reformers see no need for teachers to be rigorous scholars. Indeed, the No Child Left Behind reforms demand disempowered teachers who do what they're told and often read pre-designed scripts to their students. I am assuming in *Critical Constructivism* that such actions are insulting to the teaching profession and are designed ultimately to destroy the concept of public education itself. The study of constructivism and critical constructivism induces us to ask important questions: What is the purpose of schools? How do we organize them for maximum learning? What is the curriculum and how do we conceptualize it? How do we understand the relationship between schools and society?

Such pedagogical questions cannot be answered thoughtfully without the help of diverse theoretical knowledges. Please note that theory is defined here not as that which indicates the proper way to teach but as a body of understandings that help us make sense of education, its social and political implications, and how we as educators fit into this complex mix. In the social theoretical domain, for example, we might ask how does the existence of socio-economic inequality along the lines of race, class, gender, sexuality, religion and language influence our answers to these educational questions? What happens to our answers when we bring an understanding of power to our analytical table? What is the effect of social theoretical insight on the subjectivity and context-dependency of knowledge production? Might, for example, the knowledge emerging here help shape the way we answer questions about the curriculum? In this context we begin to understand the forces that construct knowledge. This is central to understanding constructivism and critical constructivism.

Thus, the insights of critical constructivism change the way we approach the educational act. In transmission-based conceptions of teaching there is no reason to study the learner. Teachers in such pedagogies are given the curriculum to teach. They simply pass designated knowledge along to students and then test them to see how much of it they remember. In critical constructivist schools, the identities of students matter. Children and young people enter the schoolhouse with extant worldviews, constructed by their experiences and the social contexts in which they have lived. These perspectives actively shape school experiences and learning. Indeed, they help shape all the interpretations students make about the world around them. If teachers are serious about teaching such students, critical constructivists contend, they must gain a sense of these prior perspectives and how they shape students' relationships to schooling.

Any learning must be integrated with these prior perspectives. It is a naïve view of knowledge and cognition that believes that transmitted knowledge deposited in the mind can be later taken out unchanged and uninterpreted. Such knowledges merge in complicated ways to shape idiosyncratic perspectives. Students, like all human beings, see the world from the perspective of previous experiences and knowledges. Critical constructivists study these knowledges, these interactions, and their effects. One of the reasons that I wrote *Teachers as Researchers: Qualitative Paths to Empowerment,* was because of the need for teachers to come up with systematic ways to study and understand the construction of their students' consciousnesses and their effects on their lives in schools. Without such knowledge, teachers can easily retreat into a transmission model of pedagogy (Geeland, 1996; Dougiamas, 2002).

Critical constructivists argue that traditional forms of reason and theory-as-validated-truth often contribute little to answering the most basic questions of pedagogy. How does scientific explanation help us answer the question, "What is the purpose of schools?" Social theory viewed in relation to pedagogical theory in this context profoundly enhances the ability of educators to evaluate the worth of particular educational purposes, articulations of curriculum, and evaluation practices. These theoretical modes help teachers and students escape the well-regulated administered world that unbridled rationalism and scientism work to construct. Critical constructivists use these theoretical tools to sidestep new models of social control that put a choke hold on individual and social freedom, in the process decimating teacher professionalism.

Whether we know it or not, all of us are theorists in that we develop and hold on to particular views of how things are. Such views insidiously shape our action as lovers, parents, citizens, students and teachers. Critical constructivists understand this reality and argue that the social, cognitive and educational theories we hold must be consciously addressed. Such conscious awareness allows us to reflect on our theories, explore their origins in our lives, change them when needed and consider how they may have unconsciously shaped our teaching and our actions in the world in general. Thus, we come to better understand—as great educators always should—the ways the world operates and how that operation shapes education, educational policy, curriculum, the lives of teachers and students, and who succeeds and who doesn't in schooling. Critical constructivists are painfully aware that many forces in the twenty-first century are at work to remove such insights from the realm of teaching. This book works to illustrate the importance of such understandings in the bizarre educational cosmos of the twenty-first century.

While many view constructivism and critical constructivism as theories of learning, I see them as this and much more. Constructivism/critical constructivism involves theoretical work in education, epistemology, cognition and **ontology**. In *Critical Constructivism* I argue for a unified theory where all of these dimensions fit together and are synergistic in their interrelationship. For example, it is hard to pursue a critical constructivist pedagogy without the grounding of critical constructivist epistemological and cognitive theories. In this unified context critical constructivism becomes a *weltanschauung,* a

Ontology
the branch of philosophy that studies the nature of being; that asks what it means to be in the world.

worldview that creates meaning on the nature of human existence. In this way critical constructivism comes to exert more influence in more domains than it has so far.

Point 1: Critical constructivism is grounded on the notion of constructivism. Constructivism asserts that nothing represents a neutral perspective—nothing exists before consciousness shapes it into something perceptible.

Epistemology
the branch of philosophy that studies knowledge and its production.

Positivism
an epistemological position that values objective scientific knowledge produced in rigorous adherence to the scientific method. It identifies knowledge as worthwhile to the extent that it describes objective data that reflect the world.

Bricolage
denotes a multimethodological form of research that uses a variety of research methods and theoretical constructs to examine a phenomenon.

In this context we draw upon a constructivist **epistemology** to provide insight into how the pedagogical world operates. Rejecting the rationalistic Cartesian notion that there is a monolithic knowable world "out there" explained by Western science, a constructivist epistemology (I also refer to this as an epistemology of complexity) views the cosmos as a human construction—a social construction. The world is what dominant groups of humans perceive it to be. This complicates our notion of theory. Positivistic/rationalistic theories were simple to the extent that they claimed truth-value on the basis of how they corresponded to *true* reality. More complex, post-**positivistic** theories study the various philosophical and social groundings of diverse theories, learn from them, and understand the social construction of them all. Critical constructivists take this understanding of social construction and add critical theory to the mix. Our pluralistic and multiperspectival (or as I have termed it elsewhere, **bricolage**) orientation is omnipresent, as we seek benefits from a variety of social, cultural, philosophical and theoretical positions.

An epistemology of constructivism has maintained that nothing represents a neutral perspective, in the process shaking the epistemological foundations of modernist Cartesian grand narratives. Indeed, no truly objective way of seeing exists. Nothing exists before consciousness shapes it into something we can perceive. What appears as objective reality is merely what our mind constructs, what we are accustomed to seeing. The knowledge that the world yields has to be interpreted by men and women who are part of that world. Whether we are attempting to understand the music of West Africa, the art of Marcel Duchamp, the pedagogical theory of Michael Apple, the philosophy of Jean-Paul Sartre, the lyrics of Bob Dylan or the poetry of Audre Lorde, the constructivist principle tacitly stands. For example, most analysts don't realize that the theory of perspective developed by fifteenth-century artists constituted a scientific convention. It was simply one way of portraying space and held no *absolute* validity. Thus, the structures and phenomena we observe in the physical world are nothing more than creations of our measuring and categorizing mind.

In constructivist theory, different individuals coming from diverse backgrounds will see the world in different ways. Imagine, for example, how a German bank teller, an Igbo tribesperson, a Texas rancher and a woman from a small village in China close to the Mongolian border might describe a major league baseball game. It is safe to assume that the descriptions would be quite different and even humorous to individuals who have understood the intricacies of the game since they were very young. There is no question that the backgrounds and expectations of the observer shape perception. Consider how a classroom is perceived by a class clown, a traditionally good student, a burnt-out teacher, a standardized test maker, an anti-standards activist, a bureaucratic supervisor, a disgruntled parent, a nostalgic alumnus or a student with feelings similar to the shooters, Eric and Dylan from Columbine High School. The way our psychosocial dispositions shape how the world is perceived holds important implications for teaching and critical thinking. Each of our students brings a unique disposition into the classroom. Indeed, each teacher carries a unique disposition with her or him.

In this theoretical context students of constructivism might ask:

- How are our constructions of the world shaped?
- Are our psychosocial dispositions beyond our conscious control?

- Do we simply surrender our perceptions to the determinations of our environment, our social, cultural context?
- What does this process of construction have to do with becoming an educated person?

Because people are often unable to discern the ways their environments shape their perception—i.e. is construct their consciousness—the development of modes of analysis that expose this complex process becomes very important in our critical constructivist effort. This is where the term "critical" merges with "constructivism" to form critical constructivism. Thus, we understand the origin of our term, critical constructivism. Critical theory is concerned with extending a human's consciousness of himself or herself as a social being in light of the way dominant power operates to manage knowledge. A critical theoretical analyst who gains such a consciousness would understand how his or her political opinions, religious beliefs, gender role, racial self-concept or view of the goals of education had been influenced by both the dominant culture and subcultures. Critical constructivism thus promotes reflection on the production of self. In many of the undergraduate teacher education courses I've taught over the last few decades, I have attempted to help students cultivate a critical, theoretically grounded view of the construction of their own consciousness as a prospective teacher. Why is it that I have decided to teach? What forces in my life have shaped this decision? How have these forces contributed to the type of teacher I will become?

These questions and many others combined with an introduction to critical theory initiate an introspective process that eventuates in not only self-knowledge but also in cultural and educational critique. As critical constructivist teachers study major issues in education, the students are analyzing themselves and the origins of their ways of making sense of the world. The interrelationship of these parallel studies produces some interesting perspectives, as students come to see various school purposes and reform movements play out on the terrain of their own school lives. Students come to know themselves better by using these critical theoretical insights to bring to consciousness the process by which their consciousness was constructed. Action to correct what may be viewed as harmful constructions can be negotiated once reflection reveals the psychological, ethical, moral and political foundations of the pathology.

This notion of critical constructivism allows teachers and students a critical consciousness. This involves an ability to step back from the world as we are accustomed to perceiving it and to see the ways our perception is constructed via linguistic codes, cultural signs, race, class, gender and sexual ideologies, and other often-hidden modes of power. Such ability constitutes a giant step in becoming a critical analyst, learning to be an emancipatory teacher, and assuming the role of a producer of dangerous, world-changing knowledge. Critical constructivism, thus, is a theoretically grounded form of world-making. We ask penetrating questions. How did that which has come to be, come to be? Whose interests do particular institutional arrangements serve? As critical constructivists remake and rename their world, they are constantly guided by their critical theoretical system of meaning, their emancipatory source of authority (see another of my books in the Lang Primer series, *Critical Pedagogy,* for more on this topic).

Teachers with access to critical constructivist theory, for example, are empowered to ask typically neglected questions about the socio-political purposes of schooling. In a critical theoretical context they can more clearly discern how education operates to reproduce or challenge dominant socio-political and economic structures. Such theoretical understandings are profoundly important in learning to think, teach and live democratically. Educational purpose cannot be separated from social justice, human liberation, self-direction, resistance to regulation, community building, deeper forms of human interconnection and the fight for freedom. When educators fail to gain these theoretical frames, schools inexorably become sorting machines for the new corporate order (Weil & Anderson, 2000). Without such informed modes of making meaning, schools tend to reinforce patriarchal structures, Eurocentric educational practices, homophobia and racism. The struggle for the soul of education in North America is playing out on the road before us. Critical constructivism helps us understand the ways that dominant power wielders have worked to create an educational system that benefits the most privileged at the expense of those marginalized by race, class, gender and sexuality.

Objectivism and Constructivism

There is no doubt that our concept of critical constructivism will elicit charges of educational politicization and of tainted, unobjective teaching and research with predetermined outcomes. Critical constructivism asserts that pious protestations of pseudo-objectivity must be confronted. If critical constructivists cave in to such **objectivism**, the possibility of taking a moral stand in education, of seeing education as something more than a technical act, will be destroyed. As they argue that we must keep politics out of education, objectivists misrepresent the basic tenets of critical pedagogy in general. Critics miss the point that teaching and, for that matter, research are never neutral—alas, when we attempt to remain neutral, like Pilate, we support the prevailing power structure. Thus, recognition of the ideological nature of teaching and knowledge production implies that teachers and researchers by necessity must take a position and make it explicit. They do not impose their positions or their interpretations/constructions as truth—of course, students and the researched have the right to reject everything asserted.

Objectivism the epistemological belief that disinterested knowledge can be produced about any phenomenon simply by following the scientific method.

Along with other advocates of critical pedagogy and critical research, I would maintain that noncritical, mainstream teachers and researchers are every bit as guilty of value-laden teaching and research as any critical constructivist. To assume a position which refuses to seek the structural sources of human suffering and exploitation is to support oppression and the power relations which sustain it (Freire, 1970, 1985; Perry, 2001). The arguments of objectivists that any teaching or inquiry grounded on explicit value assumptions is subjective to the point of worthlessness are similar to the nineteenth-century ruling-class idea that engaging in social criticism violates a "gentlemanly" code of civility. It is similar to a twentieth-century notion of positive thinking (cf. Dale Carnegie) that views overt oppositional behavior as a form of negativity that is not only politically incorrect but distasteful as well. Indeed, the difference between critical constructivism and objectivism rests on the willingness of critical constructivists to reveal their allegiances and to admit their solidarities, their value structures and the ways such orientations affect their work (Coben, 1998; Cary, 1998; Carlson, 1997; Carlson and Apple, 1998).

It is important to note here that objectivism is grounded on the rationalist myth of cold reason. Such cold reason asserts that knowledge is nothing more and nothing less than the scientific discovery of an external reality. This means that knowledge exists independently of our minds in a never-changing, fixed state. Thus, knowledge (and curriculum) becomes something to be delivered to passive minds. Such knowledge should be freed from human contact—it should retain the same form from the moment of production to transmission into the mind of the learner. Critical constructivism does not seek to replace objectivism with another authoritarian, certain epistemological system. Instead, it is a philosophical orientation attempting to reconceptualize the processes of thinking and knowing.

Such a reconceptualization, of course, holds profound consequences for teaching, learning, and curriculum development. Aware of the complexity of the knowledge production process and its inherent uncertainty, critical constructivism becomes an epistemology focused on the individual's process of constructing, not reflecting reality. It is a hermeneutic orientation as it views knowledge construction as an interpretive process. Such an interpretive process produces contextually specific, not universal and timeless, knowledge. Such constructivist knowledge is culturally negotiated and, unlike objectivist knowledge, is not produced by isolated individuals (Tobin, 1993; Chiari and Nuzzo, 1993; Taylor, Fraser, and White, 1994; Geeland, 1996; Dougiamas, 2002).

Cartesianisn
Rene Descartes' analytical method of reasoning, often termed "reductionism," asserted that one can appreciate complex phenomena best by reducing them to their constituent parts and then piecing the elements back together according to causal laws.

Revealing their solidarities, critical constructivists operate on the counter-**Cartesian** assumption that knower and known are inseparable. Learning from liberation theologians and critical theorists, critical constructivists embrace subjugated knowledges, in the process disallowing an objectivist subject-object dualism. When researchers respect subjugated knowledges and the unique perspective of the oppressed, they, as a matter of course, begin to subvert the relationship of domination that permeates traditional objectivist teaching and knowledge work. It is a relationship of domination that allows for both the manipulation of natural processes to serve the logic of capital (the needs of profit-making) and the manipulation of human beings as the passive objects of social engineering (McGinty, 2001). This separation of knower and known, this epistemological distancing, produces a hidden logic of domination between teacher-student, researcher-researched and knower-known; not content to occupy only the terrain of inquiry, this logic trespasses into the domain of race, class and gender relations (Fee, 1982). Indeed, it is the logic of hierarchy and authoritarianism, not democracy and inclusion.

Operating within this domain of Cartesian logic, schooling and research have often served the interests of power elites. Critical constructivism, with its commitment to the perspective of the oppressed, seeks to confront such consequences. The view of the objectivist paradigm from above gives way to views from below. Emerging from an understanding and respect for subjugated knowledge, such an epistemological position not only boasts ethical assets but holds scientific benefits as well. The scientific dimension revolves around the hierarchical relationship of researcher and researched; much of the information gathered by traditional methods is irrelevant because the subordinates being researched, realizing their inferior position, often develop a profound distrust of the researchers interrogating them.

Oppressed groups interviewed by researchers from a higher social stratum often provide expected information rather than authentic data. Critical constructivism's respect for subjugated knowledge helps construct a research situation where the experience of the marginalized is viewed as an important way of seeing the socio-educational whole, not simply as a curiosity to be reported. Such a research perspective is counter-**hegemonic** (i.e., a threat to entrenched power) and radically democratic as it uses the voice of the subjugated to formulate a reconstruction of the dominant educational structure. It is a radical reconstruction in the sense that it attempts to empower those who are presently powerless (Mies, 1982; Connell, 1989; Kincheloe, Steinberg and Villaverde, 1999).

hegemonic
the process by which dominant groups seek to impose their belief structures on individuals for the purpose of solidifying their power over them. Thus, hegemony seeks to win the consent of the governed to heir own subjugation without the use of coercion or force.

Uncovering Elitist Assumptions in the Construction of Knowledge

With this reconstructive imperative in mind, one of the central tasks of a critical constructivist teacher-scholar is to formulate questions that expose the conditions that promote social and educational advantage and disadvantage (Brosio, 1994, 2000). For example, it is obvious to many that when the methods of evaluation of advocates of the competitive, top-down standards curriculum are employed, nonwhite and working-class students do not generally do well—their performance is interpreted as a manifestation of slowness, of inferior ability (Kincheloe, Steinberg and Gresson, 1996). Researchers devise tests to evaluate school, student and teacher performance, forgetting throughout the process that evaluation is based on uncritically grounded constructions of intelligence and performance (Owen and Doerr, 1999).

Critical constructivists know that the advantage of subjugated perspectives, the view from below, involves what has been termed the "double consciousness" of the oppressed (Steinberg, 2001; King and Mitchell, 1995; Brown and Davis, 2000). If they are to survive, subjugated groups need to develop an understanding of those who control them (e.g., slaves' insight into the manners, eccentricities and fears of their masters). At the same time they are cognizant of the everyday mechanisms of oppression and the way such technologies shape their consciousness, their lived realities. Because of their privileged class, race and gender positions, many educators are insulated from the benefits of the double consciousness of the subjugated and are estranged from a visceral appreciation of suffering (Zappulla, 1997). Contemporary social organization, thus, is viewed through a lens that portrays (constructs) it as acceptable.

Why would such educators/researchers challenge research methods, modes of interpretation, and teaching strategies that justify the prevailing system of education? (Mayers, 2001a, 2001b; Jardine, 1998; Ellis, 1998; Malewski, 2001a, 2001b). What lived experiences would create an ethical dissonance within the minds of such individuals that would make them uncomfortable with the status quo? The oppressed—while often manipulated by mechanisms of power to accept injustice and to deny their own oppression—often use their pain as a motivation to find out what is not right and to discover alternative ways of constructing social and educational reality (Mies, 1982; Jaggar, 1983). Serious consideration of such subjugated ways of knowing transforms forever our conceptions of the relation of the knower to the known and the conceptualization and execution of the research act. The theoretical frames that help critical constructivists make sense of the world are intimately tied to these different ways of knowing. The questions we ask as critical constructivists often find their source in these subjugated epistemologies. Such questions consistently work to expose the elitism that shapes knowledge, the purposes of schooling, the curriculum, and who qualifies as an educated person. Such critical constructivist-based questions can reveal insights that change the world.

Point 2: Knowledge of the world is an interpretation produced by people who are a part of that world. Thus, understanding the nature of interpretation is a central feature of being an educated person.

The study of interpretation in traditional objectivist scholarship was deemed irrelevant. With the coming of the Scientific Revolution in the 1600s and the 1700s in Western Europe, knowers were separated from the known. Existing outside of time and space, scientific knowers could know the world objectively. Thus, they were untainted by the world of opinions, perspectives or values. Operating objectively (without bias), the knower embarks on the disinterested mission of science—the application of reason to the understanding of the environment. There would be no reason for critical constructivism in such a cosmos. There would be no reason to study the knower and the cultural and historical forces that shaped his or her constructions of the world. Indeed, the knowledge produced by knowers who followed the scientific method was not a construction—it was truth. No interpretation was needed in such a heady context.

Subverting the Need for Interpretation: The Scourge of Reductionism

This system of truth production took place within Rene Descartes' separation of mind and matter, his *cogito, ergo sum*— "I think, therefore I am." This view led to a conception of the world as a mechanical system divided into two distinct realms: 1) an internal world of sensation, and 2) an objective world composed of natural phenomena. Building on the Cartesian dualism, scientists argued that laws of physical and social systems could be uncovered objectively by researchers operating in isolation from human perception with no connection to the act of perceiving. The internal world of mind and the physical world, Descartes theorized, were forever separate, and one could never be shown to be a form of the other (Lavine, 1984; Lowe, 1982; Aronowitz, 1988, 1996). We understand now that this division of mind and matter had profound and unfortunate consequences—especially in questions of education. In all disciplinary domains and especially in education and psychology, this reductionistic science worked to produce oversimplified and misleading pictures of these domains. Such research produced a "thin content" and trivialized education. Education was trivialized in that the role of the teacher involved passing "certified truths" along to passive students whose role was generally to commit such unexamined truths to memory. This perspective of what a "rigorous" education involves is still promoted by conservatives in the twenty-first century.

Contributing to the victory of reductionism and its production of thin content masquerading as truth was Sir Isaac Newton. Newton extended Descartes' theories with his description of space and time as absolute regardless of context—an assertion Einstein would demolish in 1905 with a far more complex view of physical reality (see Kincheloe, Steinberg and Tippins, 1999). Clarifying the concept of cause and effect, Newton established modernism's tenet that the future of any aspect of a system could be predicted with absolute certainty if its condition was understood in precise detail and the appropriate tools of measurement were employed. Thus, the Cartesian-Newtonian concept of scientific modernism was established with its centralization, concentration, accumulation, efficiency and fragmentation. Bigger became better as the dualistic way of seeing reinforced a rationalistic, patriarchal and expansionist social and political order welded to the desire for power and conquest. Such a way of seeing served to despiritualize and dehumanize, as it focused attention on concerns other than the sanctity and well-being of people (Fosnot, 1988).

Exploring these origins of Western scientific modernism, critical constructivists maintain that we can better understand how "what is" came to be, how education and schooling took their form. Continuing in this context, Descartes and Newton, along with Francis Bacon who established the supremacy of reason over imagination, laid a foundation that allowed science and technology to change the world. Commerce increased; nationalism grew; human labor was measured in terms of productivity; nature was dominated, and European civilization gained the power to conquer in a way previously unimagined. This is the aspect of the modernist Scientific Revolution that we hear about in the subject matter of school. The problems of reductionism and rationalism are rarely referenced in such content knowledge. The rise of modernist science was closely followed by a decline in the importance of religion and spirituality. An obsession with progress supplied new objectives and values to fill the vacuum left by the loss of religious faith. Even familial ties were severed as the new order shifted its allegiance to the impersonal concerns of commerce, industry and bureaucracy (Aronowitz and Giroux, 1991; Bohm and Peat, 1987).

Rationality was deified, and around the scientific pantheon the credo of modernity was developed: the world is rational (logocentric), and there is only one meaning of the term. All natural phenomena can be painted within the frame of this monolithic rationality, whether we are studying gravity, rainbows, street gangs or teaching. The victory of reductionism was almost complete—nothing complex was noted in the relationship of the knower to the known. Reductionism remains dominant to this day, mowing down all challenges—not the critical constructivist challenge I hope—with charges of irrationality and antiscientific perspectives. It's important to note that perspectives advocating recognition of complexity and the constructed nature of knowledge have made some inroads over the last fifteen years. Such success, however, has been met with a bellicose reaction from the defenders of the positivistic/reductionistic faith. We see that fight in the first decade of the twenty-first century in the passage of No Child Left Behind legislation and the top-down imposition of content standards. In this context, critical constructivism and the contextualized view of school knowledge it promotes will not be welcomed by reductionists in educational leadership positions.

Such leaders and their allies who advocate standardized forms of educational reform do not question the Cartesian-Newtonian-Baconian premise that first and foremost science is a "fact" provider—facts that need no interpreting. Scientific research provides us, they insist, with indisputable knowledge. In this epistemological universe, values are subjective opinions that have little role in world research and education. Operating on these premises, scientific managers have objectified the teaching workplace, focusing on measurable factors related to the bottom line of productivity. The examination of human values as represented by John Dewey's assertion that education must be pursued as an ethical imperative does not fit into a view of education based on such a reductionistic notion of science. Why all this fuss about complexity, reductionism, knowledge production and epistemology, advocates of reductionism ask, when we all know that science has simply provided us with the truth? The job of teachers is simple, they tell the world. Just deliver the truth to students. The talk about interpretation is a silly waste of time.

The Power of Interpretation: Understanding Critical Hermeneutics

Engaging in critical constructivism always involves the interpretive act, making sense of the complexity of everyday life and the data it constantly throws at us. Critical constructivists are profoundly appreciative of the power of critical hermeneutics. If hermeneutics involves the act of interpretation, then critical hermeneutics involves understanding how power inscribes the word and the world to shape the nature of how human beings make sense of it. In other words, critical hermeneutics is directly concerned with how power enters into the interpretive act. Critical constructivists start with the premise that all being in the world of human beings is an interpreted form of being. This holds profound epistemological implications, as all knowledge is socially constructed in a dialogue between the world and human consciousness. Educators who understand that knowledge and interpretation are inseparable terms work to enhance their interpretive ability. Indeed, the ability to generate rich and compelling interpretations is a key to producing more rigorous forms of knowledge and pedagogy.

Long concerned with the theory and practice of interpretation, hermeneutics is a form of philosophical inquiry that focuses on the cultural, social, political and historical nature of research. Hermeneutics maintains that meaning-making cannot be quarantined from where one stands or is placed in the web of social reality. Thus, in a hermeneutic context, interpretation is denaturalized in the sense that certain events and/or phenomena do not imply a particular interpretation of their meaning. Interpretation is far more complex than reductionists assumed, far more a product of social forces than Cartesians admitted.

Thus, critical constructivists focus great attention on the act of interpretation in research, appreciating the distinction between describing a phenomenon and understanding it. Informed by hermeneutics, critical constructivists understand that any act of rigorous knowledge production involves:

- Connecting the object of inquiry to the many contexts in which it is embedded
- Appreciating the relationship between researcher and that being researched
- Connecting the making of meaning to human experience
- Making use of textual forms of analysis while not losing sight that living and breathing human beings are the entities around which and with which meaning is being made
- Building a bridge between these forms of understanding and informed action
- Understanding that rigorous teaching always involves applying these concepts to any subject matter engaged in the classroom.

Critical hermeneutics has engaged in a dialogue with the tradition of critical theory. Extending our previous conversation about critical theory, it is always concerned with the ways power operates and the ways various institutions and interests deploy power in the effort to survive, shape behavior and gain dominance over others, or, in a more productive vein, improve the human condition. Realizing that power is not simply one important force in the social process, critical theory understands that humans are the historical products of power. Men and women do not emerge outside the process of history. Human identities are shaped by entanglements in the webs that power weaves. Critical hermeneutics emerges in the dialogue between hermeneutics and critical theory's concern with power and social action (Jardine, 1998; Kincheloe, Steinberg and Villaverde, 1999; Smith, 1999; McLaren, 2000).

In this hybrid context, critical hermeneutics pushes interpretation to new levels, moving beyond what is visible to the **ethnographic** eye to the exposure of concealed motives that move events and shape everyday life. As critical hermeneutics observes the intersection of power and omnipresent, prereflective cultural meanings, a sensitive and rigorous understanding of the social world begins to take shape. Critical hermeneutics takes the concept of **historicity** to a new conceptual level, as it specifies the nature of the historicity that helps produce cultural meaning, the consciousness of knowledge producers and teachers, the construction of the research and teaching processes, and the formation of human subjectivity and transformative action. In this interpretive context critical theoretical concerns with **praxis**-based notions of social change are more easily addressed, as social action informed by thick description and rigorous understanding of a social and political circumstance is made possible (Lutz, Jones and Kendall, 1997; Zammito, 1996). In this critical hermeneutic process we begin to get down to the forces that move events. We begin to uncover what schools and other social institutions hide about how the world actually works. What we learn in this

Ethnography
a form of social and cultural research that attempts to gain knowledge about a particular culture, to identify patterns of social interaction, and to develop interpretations of societies and social institutions.

Historicity
the human state of being in the world, our place in space and time and the way it shapes us.

Praxis
an activity that combines theory and practice, thought and action for emancipatory ends.

context can be quite disconcerting—but why bother learning at all if we're not trying to get an honest picture of the phenomena in question?

In the first decade of the twenty-first century we are far better acquainted with these interpretive dynamics than we were before the paradigmatic changes of the last four decades.

The arguments put forward in this paradigm shift assert that:

- There is a distinction between the world and our linguistically driven interpretive perception of it.
- Eurocentric/American, patriarchal and elite class inscriptions can be found on most of what schools reference as "validated knowledge."
- All phenomena can be viewed from multiple vantage points—perspectives gained from these vantage points change the ways we understand phenomena.
- There will always be new and unanticipated vantage points from which to view the world—thus, meaning is not as stable as we once imagined.
- All knowledge is part of larger processes that are in flux—as the process evolves, the knowledge once thought to be stable changes along with it.

While many scholars have come to understand these paradigmatic dynamics, such a change should by no means be seen as universal. As previously maintained, there is still tremendous resistance to such a new way of thinking about knowledge and, in turn, education. Hermeneutics promotes a **dialectical** notion of understanding that seeks to free knowledge production from the authoritarian explanations of the certified experts—whether they are the religious elite of the medieval period or the scientific elite of modernity. In the modernist context hermeneutics resists scientific explanations that reduce the world to what is objectifiable, i.e., expressible in mathematical terms. This focus on understanding and interpretation rejects unilateral experiences of all kinds

Dialectics understands that knowledge is not complete in and of itself. It is produced in a larger process and can never be understood outside of its historical development and its relationship to other information.

that too often eventuate in oppression via the hyperrationalization of lived experience. Such explanations are couched in the monologic of correct and incorrect answers—a way of researching that subverts critical analysis as it imposes meanings. Such material is packaged for easy consumption. No interpretative activity is necessary, just throw it in the explanatory microwave, heat, and insert into one's memory.

Semiotics
the study of the nature and influence of signs, symbols and codes.

Hermeneutic understanding, unlike rationalist, reductionist explanation, does not launch a preemptive strike against other ways of producing knowledge. When I argue in *The Sign of the Burger: McDonald's and the Culture of Power* (2002) that McDonald's can be understood as a **semiotic** phenomenon in its strategic deployment of cultural signifiers, this does not mean that George Ritzer's McDonaldization thesis is wrong. Indeed, the two ways of interpreting McDonald's seem to me quite synergistic. Critical hermeneutics asserts that meaning is consistently multiple in nature (Reason and Bradbury, 2000; Madison, 1988; Lester, 2001). In a culture infiltrated with the ideology of the superiority of scientific explanation, such multiplicity seems to many inherently lacking in standards.

Thus, critical constructivist scholar-teachers informed by hermeneutics become rigorous researchers of context, perspective and discourse. Drawing on the concept of bricolage, they understand that they must use multiple research traditions and theoretical tools to understand the way these factors influence how we make sense of the world around us. Bricoleurs appreciate that any research that fails to account for these dynamics cannot produce a complex, thick and textured picture of a phenomenon. Empirical, quantitative studies that take these factors into account move toward the criteria of rigor. Teachers who understand these dynamics move toward a new realm of educational quality as they break free from the reductionism that stupidifies in the name of edifying.

Point 3: Interpretations cannot be separated from the interpreter's location in the web of reality—one's inter-

pretive facility involves understanding how historical, social, cultural, economic and political contexts construct our perspectives on the world, self and other.

The knowledge that critical constructivist researchers produce is grounded on the assumption that the world is shaped by a complicated, web-like configuration of interacting forces. Knowledge producers, like everyone else, are inside, not outside, the web. As previously mentioned, the knower and the known are inseparable—they are both a part of the complex web of reality. No one in this web-like configuration of the universe can achieve a godlike perspective—no one can totally escape the web and look back at it from afar. Indeed, critical constructivists argue that we all must confess our subjectivity; we must recognize our limited vantage points.

To recognize how our particular view of the web shapes our conception of social, psychological and educational reality, we need to understand our historical location. Reductionistic, cause-effect educational research tends to ignore the way our historicity works to construct our consciousness; as a result, our concept of social activity and of the educational process is reduced to a static frame. Traditional reductionistic forms of curriculum development ignore this web of reality and its impact on the production of knowledge. Curriculum and instruction in this context are delivered to passive students as truth, as free from construction by human beings from particular points in this web of reality.

Thus freed from a spatial and temporal location in the world, the reductionistic, positivistic researcher feels empowered to make predictions, to settle questions, to ignore the dialectical process in which all social activity is grounded. From this perspective, linear mathematics controls variables, eliminates extraneous perturbations, and paints a Norman Rockwell portrait of the schoolhouse (Doll, 1989; Slaughter, 1989; Capra, 1996; Lemke, 1993, 1995). Obviously, the type of knowledge and curricula produced by reductionistic science is very different from the information produced by critical constructivist educational researchers. This is a point missed in most discussions about education—where does the knowledge of school come from? What are the assumptions embedded within it? What roles do such knowledges play in shaping our consciousness?

From the perspective of Ilya Prigogine, the 1977 Nobel Prize winner in chemistry and proponent of complexity and chaos theories, reductionist, pseudo-linear science distorts the knowledge we construct about the world (Prigogine and Stengers, 1984). Prigogine and the analysts of complexity realize that pseudo-linear simplicity does not work. A so-called extraneous perturbation (an outside change), falling into the complex interactions that we have referred to as the web of reality, can produce an expanding, exponential effect. Inconsequential entities can have a profound effect in a nonlinear universe. The shape of the physical and social world depends on the smallest part. The part in a sense is the whole, for via the action of any particular part, the whole in the form of transformative change may be seen.

To exclude such considerations is to miss the nature of the interactions that constitute reality. Critical constructivism's complex reconceptualization of research and the knowledge it produces does not mean that we simplistically reject all quantitative forms of empirical science. Many questions in the world and in education involve counting, figuring percentages, averages, means, modes and so on. It does mean, however, that we conceive of such empirical questions as one part of the web of reality, that is, the interactive configuration of the world around us. A critical constructivist reconceptualization of knowledge production means recognizing, as John Dewey did decades ago, that the knower and the known are intimately connected, that a science that separates fact from value, purpose and belief is a pseudo-science divorced from the complex, lived world of human consciousness. Such a reconceptualization reminds knowledge producers that we can display our content and argue for its value but always with hesitation, a stutter, a tentativeness—

never as the final truth (Besag, 1986; Doll, 1989; Briggs and Peat, 1989; Lemke, 1993, 1995; Aronowitz, 1988, 1996; Kincheloe, 2003).

So why bother with all of these issues of constructivism, epistemology, research and **complexity theory** in something as simple as teaching skeptics may ask. The reason is that all of these features tacitly shape the nature of public conversation about teaching, and they covertly shape how all of us view the purpose of schools. The models of teaching we are taught, the definitions of research that support our inquiry, the angles from which we view intelligence, and the modes of learning that shape the way we think all emerge from these issues of knowledge production. Like reality itself, schools and classrooms are complex webs of interactions, codes and signifiers in which both teachers and students are interlaced. Just as complexity theory asserts that there is no single, privileged way to see the world, there is no one way of seeing the classroom, seeing intelligence, or seeing teacher or pupil success. In the present era of top-down standards and standardized instruction, there is one and only one correct way to see all of these concerns. Critical constructivists find that frightening and socially destructive.

Complexity theory posits that the interaction of many parts gives rise to characteristics not to be found in any of the individual parts. In this context complexity theory studies the rules shaping the emergence of these new characteristics and the self-organization of the system that develops in this autopoietic (self-creating) situation.

Critical Constructivism, Context and Complexity

On one level, the notion of the web of reality is merely a metaphorical way to describe the importance of context in the construction of knowledge and human consciousness. The more we understand the various contexts in which teaching and learning take place, the more we appreciate the complexity of the processes. The more of these contexts with which educators are familiar, the more rigorous teaching and learning become. I am not arguing here for rigor for rigor's sake. The problems of teacher education are multi-dimensional and are always embedded in a context. The more work critical constructivists studying cognition produce, the more it becomes apparent that a large percentage of student difficulties in school result not as much from cognitive inadequacy as from social contextual factors (Wertsch, 1991; Lave and Wenger, 1991; Kincheloe, Steinberg and Gresson, 1996; Kincheloe, Steinberg and Villaverde, 1999; Snook, 1999). Teachers need a rich understanding of the social backgrounds of students, the scholarly context in which disciplinary and counter-disciplinary knowledges are produced and transformed into subject matter and the political context which helps shape educational purpose.

In positivistic schools, learners' lives are decontextualized. When we examine the contexts and relationships connecting learner, culture, teaching, knowledge production and curriculum, teachers are moving into a more complex paradigm. In this "zone of complexity," learning is viewed more as a dynamic and unpredictable process. As a complex, changing, unstable system, it resists generalized pronouncements and universal steps detailing "how to do it." Complex systems interact with multiple contexts and possess the capacity for self-organization and creative innovation. Each teaching and learning context has its unique dimensions that must be dealt with individually. Our understanding of educational purpose is also shaped by the complexity of these contextual appreciations. Teacher-educators who are aware of this complexity embrace an evolving notion of purpose ever informed and modified by encounters with new contexts (Capra, 1996; Schubert, 1998; Kincheloe and Weil, 2001).

Critical constructivist teachers act on these contextual insights to not only help understand the various educational knowledges but to grasp the needs of their students. In the critical constructivist orientation, such concerns can never be separated from the socio-political context: macro in the sense of the prevailing ***Zeitgeist***; and micro as it refers to the context immediately surrounding any school. Critical constructivist teachers listen for marginalized voices and learn about their struggles with their environments. As such, teacher-educators delineate the contextual effects of the contemporary political context shaped by corporations and economic interests; they build deep relationships with local com-

Zeitgeist
German word for spirit of the times.

munities, community organizations and concerned individuals in these settings. With this in place, students gain new opportunities to learn in not only classrooms but in unique community learning environments. Here they can often address particular socio-political dynamics and learn about them in very personal and compelling ways (Vavrus and Archibald, 1998; Thomson, 2001; Grimmett, 1999; Cochran-Smith, 2000; Hoban and Erickson, 1998).

Critical constructivist teachers place great emphasis on the notion of context and the act of contextualization in every aspect of their work. When problems in their teaching arise, they stand ready to connect the difficulty to a wider frame of reference with a wide array of possible causes. When pedagogical problems fail to meet the criteria of an archetype, these teachers research unused sources and employ the information acquired to develop a larger understanding of the interaction of the various systems involved with the problem. When teachers fail to perform such an act of contextualization, students get hurt.

For example, a student who is doing poorly in school may be viewed as lacking intelligence. Upon contextualization, teachers may find that the student is disturbed by a problem at home or by an undiagnosed illness. His or her lack of academic success may have nothing to do with the question of ability. When teachers do not contextualize, they tend to isolate various parts of a pedagogical circumstance and call each a problem (Bohm and Edwards, 1991). They tinker with components of the problem but never approach its holistic nature. Educational data, for example, derive meaning only in the context created by other data. Context may be more important than content. These insights change the way educational professionals approach their work.

As is often the case, John Dewey wrote decades ago of these contextual dynamics. In the second decade of the twentieth century, Dewey observed that many thinkers see knowledge as self-contained, as complete in itself. Knowledge, he contended, could never be viewed outside the context of its relation-

Postformalism
a socio-cognitive theory that blurs boundaries separating cognition, culture, society, epistemology, history, psychoanalysis, economics and politics.

Technicalization
the focus on technique or how to do things rather than why to do things.

ship to other information. We only have to call to mind, Dewey suggested, what passes in our schools as acquisition of knowledge to understand how it is decontextualized and lacks any meaningful connection to the experience of students. Anticipating the notion of a critical constructivism and a **postformal** cognition, Dewey concluded that an individual is a sophisticated thinker to the degree to which he or she sees an event not as something isolated "but in its connection with the common experience of mankind" (Dewey, 1916, pp. 342–43). To overcome the reductionism that has plagued education and allowed for its **technicalization** and **hyperrationalization**, critical constructivist educators must take Dewey's insights into account.

Critical constructivism and the development of a consciousness of complexity

Hyperrationalization
the application of reason alone to analyses of the world in lieu of emotion, affect and concerns of worth and justice.

Understanding the importance of the web of reality and its larger connection to the importance of context leads critical constructivists to a consciousness of complexity. A consciousness of complexity involves gaining an understanding of the complexity of the world. Such a consciousness appreciates the fact that:

- Things-in-the-world often involve far more than what one notices at first glance.
- Things that appear isolated and fixed are parts of larger, ever-changing processes.
- The way one perceives an object may change dramatically when one encounters it in another context.
- Knowledge of the world is always shaped by the position of the knowledge producer.
- Ignoring relationships that connect ostensibly dissimilar objects may provide us with a distorted view of them.
- Windows into revolutionary new understandings may be opened by exploring the contradictions and asymmetries of the social, physical, psychological and educational spheres.

- Profound insights may be gained by attending to the experiences of those who have suffered as a result of a particular social arrangement or institutional organization.

These features of a consciousness of complexity move us to a higher-order thinking, a new level of awareness.

Teachers, students and educational leaders who develop such a consciousness can reshape their scholarly lives. In the process they can take charge of their own learning and refuse to be passive recipients of knowledge produced within the culture of the technical expert. When teachers gain a consciousness of complexity, they are ready to not only model such a consciousness for students but also to assess whether their school districts, schools and classrooms are working toward such an appreciation of complexity. In this context they can decide whether or not districts, schools and individual teachers are getting the help they need to enact a critical constructivist pedagogy. In this way teachers with a consciousness of complexity can design rigorous and creative forms of assessment that go far beyond the grading system and standardized-test-based school assessments now being used. Such teachers would view assessment as just one more topic to research. Using their sophisticated research and knowledge work abilities, teachers could ask a variety of questions about the workings of schools that would provide insights into school quality and, most importantly, practical understandings to be used in improving teaching in specific contexts (Zeno, 1998; Marzano and Kendall, 1999).

One of the most important features of higher-order cognition in general and critical constructivism in particular involves an awareness of and comfort with ambiguity and uncertainty. Part of a consciousness of complexity involves an awareness of the "complexity of self-production" or the multiple dimensions of our identities. This form of knowledge helps teachers understand where their views of educational purpose and teaching come from and what socio-cultural forces have made them who they are (have constructed them). With such understandings, teachers and students can consciously decide who they want to be, how they themselves view the teaching, learning, and knowledge producing processes. In relation to this self-awareness and the accompanying quest for self-direction, a consciousness of complexity involves the analysis of ethical questions of purpose. In this process, those seeking self-direction become focused on the effort to develop a moral compass to help guide their quest for empowerment. Such a compass does not always point in the same direction, as it is a pathfinding device aware of ambiguity and the need for contextual awareness (Progler, 2001).

Thus, the direction, it gives—much like the message, from the gods Hermes delivered to mortals—are always subject to interpretation. As hermeneutics informs us, the actions in the world such interpretations suggest are never clear cut and obvious. Again, a consciousness of complexity does not mean that we fall into an impotent relativism where courageous action in the world is subverted. Instead, our actions are informed by multiple perspectives and ways of seeing, insights that empower teachers, students and educational leaders to act in thoughtful, reflective, moral and just ways. With such a consciousness, teachers can make decisions and take actions that include all participants in the quest for a socially just, inclusive, rigorous and useful education. The cognitive alienation inherent in viewing things-in-themselves, being directed to isolate objects of study from the larger contexts and processes of which they are a part is challenged by a consciousness of complexity (Karunaratne, 1997). Critical constructivism, of course, promotes the cultivation of such a consciousness.

Teachers and students deploying a consciousness of complexity learn logics of argumentation, modes of developing compelling interpretations, and other ways of thinking more clearly. As teachers work to cultivate such higher orders of cognition, they provide students with alternative modes of meaning-making and new universes of choices in the effort to answer questions about the social and physical worlds. Such teaching can begin early in a child's schooling as early childhood and elementary teachers engage in analytical activities similar to the types outlined in the philosophy-for-children programs. Expert teachers operating in this critical constructivist context use their research skills to construct such rigorous learning activities as seamless parts of the everyday lives of their students. At their best, these expert teachers design higher-order academic lessons that are so natural to their students' lives, they don't even know they're engaged in rigorous learning (Newland, 1997).

Learning proceeding in this context as a natural part of living sets the affective stage for problem-detecting and problem-solving, the acquisition of important content, and the exposure of limiting assumptions such as, "that's just the way school is, there's nothing we can do about it." Operating in such a comfortable setting, students learn to be researchers as a normal part of their lives, they learn to use abilities acquired in a previous context in a new domain. Contrast such pedagogies and forms of consciousness with those promoted by top-down technical standards and other reductionistic pedagogies. In critical-constructivist-driven pedagogy, the atmosphere of the school changes, the disposition of students toward learning is revolutionized, the dignity of the profession of teaching is resuscitated, and the educational expectations for teachers and students are significantly raised (Newland, 1997). The school environment transmogrifies from one of punitive memory work to one of an exciting pursuit of a consciousness of complexity. Such a consciousness allows teachers and learners to analyze, understand and act intelligently in new situations.

Point 4: The "critical" in critical constructivism comes from critical theory and its concern with extending a human's consciousness of herself as a social being—critical theory promotes self-reflection in relation to social power and its ability to align our self-perceptions and world views with the interests of power blocs.

Critical constructivism is grounded on the Frankfurt School's formulation of critical theory, in particular, its attempt to explore how consciousness is tied to history. Guided by such concerns, critical constructivist teachers and researchers inspired by critical theory seek to expose what constitutes reality for themselves and for the participants in educational situations (Kincheloe and McLaren, 2000; Hinchey, 1998; McLaren, 2000). How do these participants, critical constructivist teachers ask, come to construct their views of educational reality? Critical constructivist action researchers see a socially constructed world and ask what are the forces that construct the consciousness, the ways of seeing of the actors who live in it? Uncritical researchers attempt to provide accurate portrayals of educational reality, but they stop short of analyzing the origins of the forces that construct actor consciousness. Without such information, critical constructivist teacher researchers maintain, emancipatory action is impossible. Descriptions of educational reality outside the boundaries of the socio-economic cultural context hold little meaning for educators concerned with social justice and ethical action.

Why are some constructions of educational reality embraced and officially legitimized by the dominant culture while others are repressed? (McLaren, 1989; Lincoln and Guba, 1985; Denzin and Lincoln, 2000). This is the type of question that critical teachers/researchers seek to answer. Indeed, the essence of critical constructivism concerns the attempt to move beyond the formal style of thinking which emerged from empiricism and rationalism, a form of cognition which solves problems framed by the dominant paradigm, the conventional way of seeing. Like Einstein's physics, critical constructivist researchers attempt to use their understanding of the social construction of reality to rethink and reconceptualize the types of questions we ask about the educational enterprise (Yeakey, 1987; Noblit, 1984, 1999; Kincheloe, Steinberg and Tippins, 1999; Willinsky, 2001a, 2001b).

Constructing a Critical System of Meaning

A central theme of these reconceptualized questions involves the inquiry into whose constructions of reality prevail and whose ought to prevail. Michael Young (1971) argues that the dominant definitions, the official ways of seeing in schools, are constructed realities that benefit some groups and not others. The ways that schools distinguish bright from stupid, good citizenship from bad, model behavior from disruptiveness, good work from bad work, are constructions that emanate from those in a position to induce less privileged actors to grant their consent to the dominant definitions. Much of the inquiry into education commences without an attempt to construct a system of meaning on which to ground analysis of the questions it pursues—it merely accepts the unproblematized assumptions of mainstream scholarship and research. Even when we do attempt to construct a system of meaning to ground our inquiry, it may be intellectually immature if we neglect an analysis of the hidden ideological forces that define our methodology, shape our logic, anesthetize our ethical sense and shape our questions. Without attention to such concerns, our inquiries lapse into an irrelevancy and a myopia that constrain the educational possibilities offered by empowered, insightful teachers (Yeakey, 1987; Cochran-Smith and Lytle, 1993, 1998).

Thus, teachers and scholars informed by critical theory seek a system of meaning that grants a new angle, a unique insight into the social consequences of different ways of knowing, different forms of knowledge and different approaches to research. Inquiry and the knowledge it produces are never neutral but are constructed in specific ways that privilege particular logics and voices while silencing others. Why do science and math curricula in the United States, for example, receive more attention and prestige in public schools than liberal arts? (Brown, 2001; Barton and Osborne, 2001; Roth, Tobin and Ritchie, 2001). Critical constructivists searching for the way power helps shape individual and social consciousness uncover links between the need of large corporations to enhance worker productivity and the goals of contemporary educational reform and standards movements to reestablish "excellent" schools (Horn, 2000; Horn and Kincheloe, 2001). They discover relationships between the interests of business and the exclusion of the study of labor history from Western schools (Kincheloe, 1995, 1999). They expose the connections between the patriarchal Eurocentrism of educational leadership and definitions of classics that exclude the contributions of women, minorities, and non-Westerners to the literature, art, and music curricula (Powell, 2001; Rose and Kincheloe, 2003).

Power regulates discourses; discursive practices are defined as a set of tacit rules that regulate what can and cannot be said, who can speak with the blessing of authority and who must listen, whose socio-educational constructions are scientific and valid and whose are unlearned and unimportant (Lemke, 1995). In the everyday world of teachers, legitimized discourses insidiously tell teachers what books may be read by students, what instructional methods may be utilized (Madeleine Hunter, Success for All, etc.) and what belief systems, definitions of citizenship and views of success may be taught. Schools may identify, often unconsciously, conceptions of what it means to be educated with upper-middle class white culture; expressions of working class or non-white cultures may be viewed as uneducated and inferior. As a result, teachers are expected to sever students' identifications with their minority group or working class backgrounds, thereby alienating such students through the degradation of their culture.

Thus, the culture of schooling privileges particular practices and certain methods of discerning truth. Foucault argues that truth is not relative (i.e., all world views embraced by different researchers, cultures and individuals are of equal worth), but is relational (constructions considered true are contingent upon the power relations and historical context in which they are formulated and acted upon). This is a central tenet of critical constructivism. The question that grounds our attempt to formulate a critical constructivist system of meaning to ground our pedagogy and social action is, If what we designate as truth is relational and not certain, then what set of assumptions can we use to guide our activities as professionals, to inform our questions as cultural workers? (McLaren, 1989; Pinar, 1994; Rasberry, 2001).

Liberation Theology and the Critical Constructivist System of Meaning

This is why developing a system of emancipatory meaning is so important. This is why liberation theology is so central to our attempt to develop an emancipatory system of meaning. Liberation theology, with its roots deep in the Latin American struggle against poverty and colonialism, morally situates our attempt to formulate an explicit set of assumptions, an ethical starting line from which to begin our formulation of educational questions. Liberation theology makes no apology for its identification with the perspectives of those who are excluded and subjugated. Proclaiming their solidarity with the marginalized, liberation theologians work alongside them in their attempt to expose the existing social order as oppressive and unethical. All aspects of our emancipatory system of meaning and the scholarship and pedagogy that grow out of it rest on this notion of identification with the perspective of the oppressed. Accordingly, one of the main goals of critical constructivism is to reveal the ways that dominant schooling serves to perpetuate the hopelessness of the subjugated (Welch, 1985). On the basis of this knowledge, of their "dangerous memory," strategies for overcoming such oppression can be developed.

Glossary

Bricolage—The French word, *bricoleur*, describes a handyman or handywoman who makes use of the tools available to complete a task. Some connotations of the term involve trickery and cunning and are reminiscent of the chicanery of Hermes, in particular, his ambiguity concerning the messages of the gods. If hermeneutics came to connote the ambiguity and slipperiness of textual meaning, then bricolage can also imply imaginative elements of the presentation of all formal research. I use the term here in the way Norman Denzin and Yvonna Lincoln (2000) employ it in *The Handbook of Qualitative Research* to denote a multimethodological form of research that uses a variety of research methods and theoretical constructs to examine a phenomenon (see Kincheloe and Berry, 2004).

Cartesianism—the philosophy and scientific method of Rene Descartes. Descartes' analytical method of reasoning, often termed "reductionism," asserted that one can appreciate complex phenomena best by reducing them to their constituent parts and then piecing the elements back together according to causal laws.

Complexity theory—posits that the interaction of many parts gives rise to characteristics not to be found in any of the individual parts. In this context complexity theory studies the rules shaping the emergence of these new characteristics and the self-organization of the system that develops in this autopoietic (self-creating) situation. As the complex system is analyzed, complexity theorists come to understand that it cannot be reduced to only one level of description.

Dialectics—understands that knowledge is not complete in and of itself. It is produced in a larger process and can never be understood outside of its historical development and its relationship to other information.

Epistemology—the branch of philosophy that studies knowledge and its production. Epistemological questions include: what is truth? Is that a fact or an opinion? On what basis do you claim that assertion to be true? How do you know?

Ethnography—a form of social and cultural research that attempts to gain knowledge about a particular culture, to identify patterns of social interaction, and to develop interpretations of societies and social institutions. Ethnography seeks to make explicit the assumptions one takes for granted as a culture member. Ethnographic researchers make use of observation and interviews of culture members in their natural setting, their lived contexts.

Hegemonic—the process by which dominant groups seek to impose their belief structures on individuals for the purpose of solidifying their power over them. Thus, hegemony seeks to win the consent of the governed to heir own subjugation without the use of coercion or force

Historicity—the human state of being in the world, our place in space and time and the way it shapes us. Such a concept is very important in constructivist and enactivist theory.

Hyperrationalization—the application of reason alone to analyses of the world in lieu of emotion, affect and concerns of worth and justice.

Objectivism—the epistemological belief that disinterested knowledge can be produced about any phenomenon simply by following the scientific method. If the method is followed rigorously, no values, ideology or other human perspectives will undermine the objectivity/validity of the knowledge produced.

Ontology—the branch of philosophy that studies the nature of being; that asks what it means to be in the world.

Positivism—an epistemological position that values objective scientific knowledge produced in rigorous adherence to the scientific method. It identifies knowledge as worthwhile to the extent that it describes objective data that reflect the world.

Postformalism—a socio-cognitive theory that blurs boundaries separating cognition, culture, society, epistemology, history, psychoanalysis, economics and politics. Postformalism transcends much of the cognitive theory typically associated with Piagetian and many other theories of cognitive development. While more positivist cognitive science has associated disinterestedness, objectivity, adult cognition and problem solving with higher-order thinking, postformalism challenges such concepts. Postformalism links itself to the concept of alternative rationalities. These new rationalities employ forms of analysis sensitive to signs and symbols, the power of context in relation to thinking, the role of emotion and feeling in cognitive activity, and the value of the psychoanalytical process as it taps into the recesses of (un)consciousness. In the spirit of critical theory and critical pedagogy, postformalism attempts to democratize intelligence. In this activity postformalists study issues of purpose, meaning and value. Do certain forms of cognition and cognitive theory undermine the quest for justice? Do certain forms of psychological research cause observers to view problematic ways of seeing as if they involved no issues of power and privilege?

Praxis—an activity that combines theory and practice, thought and action for emancipatory ends.

Semiotics—the study of the nature and influence of signs, symbols and codes.

Technicalization—the focus on technique or how to do things rather than why to do things.

Zeitgeist—German word for spirit of the times.

CHAPTER TWO

Power and Knowledge Production

Critical Constructivist Pedagogical Purpose

Point 5: The key elements of a rigorous education involve understanding how our consciousness is constructed, subjectivity shaped, and identity produced—here rests the theoretical key to critical constructivism: the role of power in these processes of self-production and, in turn, epistemology and knowledge production.

Cartesian-Newtonian-Baconian Modernism over a period of several decades in the seventeenth and eighteenth centuries, these three thinkers laid the foundation for the western scientific way of viewing the world. Such a mode of understanding would enable scientists to both describe and control the outside world. The foundation established by Carter, Newton, and Bacon allowed science and technology to change the world.

Critical constructivists maintain that **Cartesian-Newtonian-Baconian modernism** has been trapped in an epistemology that locates truth in external reality. Teaching and producing knowledge in this context often have become little more than an effort to accurately reflect this reality. Indeed, Cartesian thought has been seen as simply an inner process conducted in the minds of autonomous (abstract) individuals. The thoughts, moods, understandings and sensations of the individuals are separate from their histories and social contexts. If thinking is to be seen as a mirroring of external events, the need for a theory of critical constructivism is as irrelevant as the need for interpretation.

In Cartesian modernism the ability to conceptualize has little to do with culture, power or discourse, or the tacit understandings unconsciously shaped by them. Moreover, from the Cartesian perspective the curriculum becomes merely a body of finalized knowledge to be transferred to the minds of students. More critical observers may contend that this is a naïve view, but the naïveté is recognizable only if knowledge formation is understood as a complex and ambiguous social activity. The human mind is more than a repository of signifieds, a mirror of nature. A critical constructivist epistemology assumes that the mind creates rather than reflects, and the nature of this creation cannot be separated from the surrounding social world (Bowers and Flinders, 1990; Kincheloe, 2001; O'Riley, 2003).

Critical constructivist knowledge emerges neither from subjects nor from objects but from but from a dialectical relationship between the knower (subject) and the known (object). Drawing from Jean Piaget, this dialectical relationship is represented by the **assimilation-accommodation dyad**. Employing these conceptualizations, critical constructivist teachers conceive knowledge as culturally produced and recognize the need to construct their own criteria for evaluating its quality. This constructivist sense-making process is a means by which teachers can explain and introduce students to the social and physical world and help them build for themselves an epistemological infrastructure for interpreting the phenomena they confront. Thus, an educated person in this context begins to construct her own meaning-making structures, her own interpretive strategies, her own criteria for producing and consuming knowledge. Critical constructivists realize that because of the social construction of knowledge, their interpretations and infrastructures are a part of the cosmos, but they are not always in the cosmos. As a result, when the recognition of need arises we can always modify our viewpoints—we can accommodate (Kaufman, 1978; Brooks, 1984; Benson, 1989;

Assimilation-Accommodation dyad
Assimilation involves the shaping of an event to fit into one's cognitive structure. Accommodation, on the other hand, refers to the restructuring of one's cognitive maps to take care of an event. To Piaget, intellectual adaptation always involves equilibration between assimilation and accommodation.

Kincheloe, 1995; Rose and Kincheloe, 2003).

Thus, the Cartesian-Newtonian-Baconian conception of truth and certainty is fundamentally questioned by the epistemology of critical constructivism. We can never apprehend the world in a "true" sense, apart from our selves and our lives. As living parts of the world we are trying to figure out, we can only approach it from the existing cognitive infrastructures that shape our consciousness. Limited in this way, we can see only what our mind allows. With this restriction we are free to construct the world any way we desire. This is not to say, however, that the outcomes of our constructions will not be confused—they may even be destructive. We may, for example, adopt a worldview such as that of the medieval Europeans. In this view of the world, sanitation was irrelevant, and thousands of individuals died as the result of the Black Plague. Obviously, this was not an adequate construction of the nature of the world. This recognition confronts us with calls to develop a way of determining valid constructions of reality. In response to such a call, critical constructivism lays out some guiding principles for judging more adequate and less adequate constructions. Critical constructions:

- *provide a richer insight into a phenomenon than do others.* Is the construction conscientious in answering all the inquiries it raises about the phenomenon? Is it sensitive to the complexity in which all phenomena are embedded? Does it expand our consciousness in relation to the phenomenon?
- *provide an interconnected and cohesive portrait of the phenomenon.* Does it delineate diverse interrelationships that construct the phenomenon? Does it illustrate the ways these interrelationships shape the form the phenomenon takes?
- *grant access to new possibilities of meaning.* Does it raise new questions and suggest new types of research into the phenomenon? Does it help in the construction of future insights?

- *benefit marginalized groups in their struggle for empowerment.* Does it elucidate the role of power in shaping the lives of those connected to the phenomenon? Does it identify where individuals are situated in the socio-political web of reality? Does it uncover the ways ideology operates to undermine individuals' desire for both self-direction and interconnectedness?
- *fit the phenomenon under study.* Are the questions raised and answered in the construction appropriate to the topic explored? Is there coherence between the analysis and the phenomenon being researched?
- *account for many of the cultural and historical contexts in which the phenomenon is found.* Does it use these contexts in the effort to make sense of the phenomenon? Does it identify the multiple processes of which the phenomenon is a part and how they shape it?
- *consider previous constructions of the phenomenon in question.* Does it point out their strengths and deficiencies? Does it place itself in this history of interpretations and constructions so the analyst understands its relationship to other interpretations and constructions? Does it examine the motives of those who have offered diverse constructions of the phenomenon?
- *generate insight gained from the recognition of the dialectic of particularity and generalization of wholes and parts.* Does it make use of the **hermeneutic circle**? Does it question the relationship between the abstract and the concrete, between socio-historical forces and individual lives? Does its engagement in the hermeneutic circle help create new metaphors that move analysis out of cliched modes? Does it reveal the impact of the unconscious use of metaphors on the interpretive process?
- *indicate an awareness of the forces that have constructed it.* Does the construction explore the place in the web of reality from which it emanates and the impact of this dynamic on the form it

Hermeneutic circle

The hermeneutic circle shifts the attention of an analyst back and forth between systems levels, connecting what might seem to some to be unrelated ideas. In the hermeneutic circle the meaning of a phenomenon begins to emerge as parts and wholes are examined in relation to one another.

assumes? Does it raise questions of self-understanding, e.g., the nature of the relationship of the producer of a text to the phenomenon in question? Does it indicate an awareness of the discourses, values and ideologies that have helped construct it?

- *make use of perspectives of multiple individuals coming from diverse social locations.* Have these voices been examined in relation to the social, linguistic, cultural and ideological forces that construct them? Does it make use of subjugated knowledges?
- *catalyze just, intelligent and worthwhile action.* Does it engage its subjects to better conceptualize the world so they can transform it? Does it recognize the specters of action implicit in the knowledge constructed (Madison, 1988; Lather, 1991, 1993)?

The Cartesian modernist view of the self cannot stand up to the epistemological assault of critical constructivism. Taking the concept of knower-known inseparability one more step, poststructuralist analysis examines the socially constructed dimensions of language and discursive practices. French social theorist Michel Foucault observed that discourse referred to a body of regulations and structures grounded in power relations that covertly shape our perspectives and insidiously mold our constructions. Russian cultural theorist and philosopher Mikhail Bakhtin complemented Foucault's observations, maintaining that power functions in a way that solidifies dominant discourses, in the process erasing the presence of unorthodox or marginal voices. Critical constructivists learn much from these theories. After Foucault and Bakhtin, the notion of the autonomous self free from the "contamination" of the social is dead; as language-utilizing organisms we cannot escape the effect of the ways discursive practices construct our ways of seeing ourselves and the world.

With these insights, critical constructivist teachers direct student attention to the study of discursive formations in the classroom. They are empowered to point out specific examples of how power shapes particular discursive formats and the ways that power subsequently works to construct consciousness (McLaren, 1995, 2000; Giroux, 1997a; Thayer-Bacon, 2001). For example, consider a critical constructivist history teacher who alerts students to the male-centered construction of American history textbooks and school district curriculum guides. The teacher uncovers an approach to teaching American history that revolves around the principles of expansionism, conquest and progress. The westward movement of America is a central organizing theme that serves to focus the gaze of the student on the "impediments to civilization," for example, natives, "unusable" land, other nations such as Mexico and England, and so on. In this context student consciousness is constructed to ignore the ethical and moral dimensions of empire building, to identify those different from us as the "other," as inferior enemies. A nationalistic consciousness is constructed that not only exonerates the sins of the past but also tends to ignore national transgressions of the present.

Critical Constructivism and the Destabilization of Fixed Meanings

The concept of civilization embedded in our history textbooks becomes what French philosopher Jacques Derrida calls a "transcendental signified"—a transhistorical fixed meaning impervious to alternate interpretations. Critical constructivists maintain that all texts, all signifiers and signifieds, are open to alternate interpretations. The construction of a text and the laws of its organization are not obvious to the prevailing wisdom, to common sense. As Derrida (1981) puts it in his book *Dissemination:* "A text is not a text unless it hides from the first comer, from the first glance, the law of its composition and the rules of its game" (p. 63). It is with the rejection of the transcendental signified (the final and intractable construction of the truth about a phenomenon) that deconstruction meets the epistemology of critical constructivism. Placing the responsibility for meaning-making squarely on human shoulders, both **deconstruction** and critical constructivism attempt to escape the hot lead enema of fixed meanings.

Deconstruction can be defined in many ways—as a method of reading, as an interpretive strategy, and as a philosophical strategy. In critical constructivism it involves all three of these definitions, as it views the world as texts to be decoded, to be explored for unintended meanings.

As Derrida informs critical constructivism's effort to prevent dominant groups from certifying their constructions as final truths, we are better equipped to resist the unwitting construction of our consciousness, the covert shaping of our subjectivity. Thus, via Derrida's deconstruction, we disrupt the tyranny of the official text—the fixing of meaning. As critical constructivists, we break the power of the author or the supervisor or the developer of educational standards or the curriculum-maker to impose authoritarian meaning (Harvey, 1989; Kincheloe, 2002). If we are unaware of Derrida's deconstruction, we are vulnerable to the mainstream seduction of the view of language as a neutral message system. This Cartesian-Newtonian-Baconian perspective regards language as a transparent medium through which students and teachers talk to one another from unproblematized abstract selves—their identities are not socially constructed; they are totally separate from the social, cultural and historical contexts in which they developed. We remain ignorant of the tacit social dimensions of language and the power dynamics it reflects in ostensibly innocent conversations.

In this context we return to the importance of interpretation in critical constructivism. Indeed, the teaching of interpretation becomes a central focus of the critical constructivist curriculum. Idiosyncratic readings protect students from "correct" interpretations and fixed meanings, as they, in the process, gain practice in recognizing the ways dominant power is attempting to construct their consciousness. Contrary to the pronouncements of some critics, all meaning is not lost by the rejection of many "correct" readings and numerous fixed meanings. If anything is destroyed in such deconstructive analysis, it is not meaning but the stance of the unchallenged superiority of one way of making meaning over all others (Zavarzadeh and Morton, 1991; Kincheloe and Weil, 2001). Indeed, the interpretative classroom discussions in which we participate should never end "for good." This is why critical constructivist teachers will study the same texts in different ways in different classes or in different semesters.

While critical constructivists are interested in diverse interpretations, like good detectives we are interested in their origins. The search for the forces that generated the interpretations and constructions of the moment move us into a great cultural conversation—the heart of the critical constructivist curriculum. Through this search, our personal experience is illuminated by our engagement in the cultural conversation and the cultural conversation is illuminated by our personal experience. We make knowledge through our actions and comments. The critical constructivist curriculum leaves us not with a sacred, never-changing set of truths but with a tentative encounter with the collective consciousness and a lingering uncertainty about the language used in the process.

The Importance of the Theoretical Domain in Critical Constructivism's Analysis of the Production of the Self

Critical constructivists maintain that researchers and educators must become well acquainted with the theoretical insights delineated here to understand the complicated dynamics of self-production. The process of meaning-making in a critical constructivist context, for example, involves engagement with texts and diverse experiences for the purpose of gaining a new level of self-understanding. Critical constructivism's effort to gain insight into personal identity is not, however, a call to narcissism; indeed, it is quite the opposite. Critical constructivists learn to understand the oppressive forces that shape them so that—especially in contemporary Western culture—they can become less self-absorbed and individually oriented. In this context they learn to situate themselves historically and socially. With such knowledge they are far better equipped to make conscious decisions about who they want to be and how they will deal with the ideological socialization processes of twenty-first century electronic- and information-saturated societies.

In many contemporary educational settings driven by unexamined top-down content standards, students and teachers are not encouraged to confront why they tend to think as they do about themselves, the world around them and their relationships to that world. In other words, such individuals gain little insight into the forces that shape them—the construction of their consciousnesses. As long as selfhood is not challenged and the status quo is accepted, such education proceeds without concern for the consequences of meaning-making. Indeed, uncritical education views cognition as a neutral process that takes place in a vacuum. Critical constructivists understand that thinking in a new way always necessitates personal transformation; if enough people think in new ways, social transformation is inevitable.

One reason this situating of self does not take place in such uncritical educational settings is that many of those involved in the educational process do not have the historical, philosophical, sociological and cultural studies backgrounds to delineate what such an act might entail. Insights derived from these domains would help educators discern the ways that dominant power subverts democratic impulses in a variety of venues, including the political, epistemological, psychological, curricular and pedagogical. Increasingly dominated by private interests, these domains operate to construct the identities of individuals in ways that were conducive to the needs of dominant power wielders. The standards-driven education of the twenty-first century attempts to make individuals more compliant with the needs of corporations, more accepting of government by the market, globalized capitalism, free-market ideologies, the irrelevance of the political domain, etc. The ideological deployment of schools as sorting mechanisms for the new corporate order is left unchallenged by this uncritical compliance. Where the self fits in these power-driven dynamics is, of course, irrelevant.

The political dynamic of self-production is central to critical constructivism. Of course, the concept of an abstract individual formed outside the boundaries of the social and cultural world is the dominant modernist conception of "self-production." The complex modes of analysis promoted by critical constructivism maintain that thinking and consciousness themselves cannot be separated from history. All thinking and action take place in continuity with the forces of history. Contextualization is inseparable from cognition and action. A key role of critical constructivism is to bring this recognition to the front burner of consciousness. With such awareness critical analysts begin to realize that consciousness is constructed by individual agency, individual will, and the ideological, discursive and regulatory influences of social forces. The self is both structured by forces and a structuring agent. Thus, "who we are" is not deterministically constructed by sociohistorical formations that totally shape our ways of seeing, nor are consciousness and selfhood autonomously constructed by free and independent individuals unhindered by the burden of history.

Human efforts to make sense of self and the world are dominated by ideological forces that thwart our pursuit of individual goals. At the same time, particular forms of thinking and action reveal a volition and a genuine motivation that transcend the confines of existing social forces. Social theorists have traditionally been guilty of not recognizing this ambiguity of consciousness construction, identity production and social action. Not until the 1980s with the influx of new theories of language analysis and cultural understanding did scholars appreciate the ways power was embedded in language and knowledge and the implications of such inscriptions in the production of the self. Human beings are initiated into language communities where women and men share bodies of knowledge, epistemologies and the cognitive styles that accompany them. These are powerful forces in the shaping of who we are. Thus, the manner in which we come to think about education and knowledge production is inseparable from these language communities. Indeed, the nature of the modes of analysis we devise is inseparable from them. Critical constructivism understands these dynamics; it understands that the sociohistorical dimensions of self-production are often manifested on the terrain of language.

These are often foreign and difficult-to-understand concepts for many students schooled in the United States. Thus, you are not unusual if you find them a bit strange and unfamiliar. But because these linguistic and ideological factors are hidden from many of us, we find ourselves removed from even thinking about the process through which our consciousness is constructed. Our educational experience has focused on the "mastery" (read: memorization) of many bits and pieces of unrelated data for standardized tests—not on the forces that have made us who we are. The schemas that guide a culture are rarely part of an individual's conscious mind. Usually, they are comprehended as a part of an individual's worldview that is taken for granted. It was these ideas that the great Italian social theorist Antonio Gramsci had in mind when he argued that philosophy should be viewed as a form of self-criticism.

In very specific terms critical constructivism is profoundly concerned with the production of self in the context of the influence of power blocs in contemporary society. Such concern reveals itself in a critical questioning of the social, cultural, political, economic, epistemological and linguistic structures that shape human consciousness as well as the historical contexts that gave birth to the structures. Such modes of analysis help students and teachers explore the sociohistorical and political dimensions of schooling, the kind of meanings that are constructed in classrooms, and how these meanings are translated into student consciousness. Naive educators often speak of student and teacher empowerment as if it were a simple process that could be accomplished by a couple of creative learning activities. One thing our ideological critique of self-production tells us is that the self is a complex, ambiguous and contradictory entity pushed and pulled by a potpourri of forces. The idea that the self can be reconstructed and empowered without historical study, linguistic analysis and an understanding of social construction is a trivialization of the goals of critical constructivism.

Critical constructivists ask the question: how do we move beyond simply uncovering the sources of consciousness construction in our larger attempt to reconstruct the self in a critical reflective manner? Grounded on their understandings of power and its influence, critical constructivists are impelled to search in as many locations as possible for alternate discourses, for ways of thinking and being that expand the envelopes of possibility. In order to engage in this aspect of the reconstruction of self, students and teachers must transcend the modernist conception of the static and unified self that goes through life with a genetically fixed I.Q. While the process of freeing oneself from this prison of the intellect is urgent, we cannot in the process neglect the search for alternate discourses in literature, history, popular culture, the community, and especially in previously devalued, subjugated knowledges. Through this process, critical constructivists develop their social and aesthetic imaginations. Here we imagine what we might become by recovering and reinterpreting what we once were. While we might use this to change our conception of the world around us, we must see this change of conception—this change of mind—as only the first step in a set of actions designed to change reality.

Cognitive Theory in Critical Constructivism—Entering the Realm of Enactivism

As critical constructivists journey through a land mystified by power, the pedagogical and social theoretical realms provide insight into our effort to reconceptualize selfhood and social institutions. A central and neglected feature of the theoretical base of critical pedagogy and critical theory involves the cognitive domain. Picking up on the work of the Santiago school of cognitive theory, we now examine enactivism in relation to critical constructivism. Indeed, Santiago's enactivism claims constructivism as an intellectual ancestor. Humberto Maturana and Francisco Varela (1987) argue in a constructivist vein that the world we know is not pre-given but enacted. Thus, the act of cognition in this context does not involve the Cartesian effort to commit to memory "*mental* reflections" of the real world. Instead of attempting to reconstruct "true" mental reflections of the "real world," learners should focus on our actions *in relation* to the world that creates them.

Of course, as we have already maintained, this notion of cognition and even learning as acts of reflecting or representing reality is a key dimension of the history of Western cognitive psychology. In this Cartesian cognitivism, sensory inputs are reconstituted by the brain in a manner that renders them as internal representations of the world "out there." Such a view of cognition produces fixed perspectives and particular viewpoints as reality itself. Conversation retreats as canons are created, and, contrary to Allen Bloom's (1987) argument, minds are closed by not moving to the margins. Critical thinkers in this cognitive theoretical domain can announce that they have deduced the truth, that they have represented reality correctly. The curriculum can thus be constructed around such truth, and everyone else can go home and "just learn it." Enactivism throws a monkey wrench into such cognitive arrogance, forcing us in the process to account for the profoundly different constructions of reality that emerge when the world is encountered in different times and places. Teaching, learning and knowledge production that do not take such cognitive complexity into account are shortchanged.

The problems of the physical, social, psychological and educational domains rarely present themselves in a well-structured, puzzle-like way.

Rationalistic technical thinking does not work very well when it confronts lived world problems that are complex and ill structured. Such situations demand more than procedural, technical reasoning. Analysts have to understand a range of tacit knowledges, the multiple contexts in which the problem is situated, and thinking processes that may or may not be of value. Educators make an important breakthrough in this context. They understand that the step-by-step procedures laid down by rationalists and the rules of rigorous research specified by positivists can hinder rather than help in the complications of the lived world. Enactivists maintain that such rules must melt away in the specificity and improvisation of immediate experience.

Looking at the concept of mind from biological and psychological perspectives, enactivists begin the reparation process necessitated by the Western rationalistic reduction and fragmentation of the world. When enactivism is added to critical constructivism's theoretical bricolage of critical theory, complexity theory, feminism, postformalism, et al., we emerge with a powerful grounding for a reconceptualized mode of meaning-making. As Jean Lave, Valerie Walkerdine, James Werstch, Etienne Wenger, Roy Pea and numerous other cognitive theorists have argued in the spirit of Russian psychologist Lev Vygotsky over the last two decades: cognition and the knowledge it produces are socially situated activities that take place in concrete historical situations. Varela adds to this description, arguing that it is in the particular historical circumstance that we realize who we are and what we can become. Indeed, we realize our cognitive capabilities in the specific concrete circumstance while concurrently gaining the power to imagine what capabilities we can develop.

At this juncture it is important to ask, what does this theorizing say to those of us in the teaching profession who want to enact a pedagogy grounded on a critical constructivist perspective? A few ideas here may be helpful. With the aid of the social, political and cognitive theories we have explored, we can begin to understand that the world in general and the educational realm in particular may be more complex than we have been taught. The key here is that teachers must become scholars who understand the multiple dimensions of the cognitive act, the reasons that it has been conceptualized so differently by different analysts at different times. Teacher-scholars begin to realize that critical teaching has to be both theoretically understood and enacted in particular circumstances. Indeed, the proof is in the concrete pudding, as teachers and students take multiple understandings into account as they improvise criticality in specific lived situations.

Following up on Enactivist Insights

Varela argues that individuals engage in a higher order of thinking when they learn to utilize knowledge and feelings from a circumstance where particular ways of thinking and acting are deemed smart, and transfer it to more complex situations where intelligent action is deemed ambiguous. Thus, intelligent behavior does not involve a form of reasoning where universal rules are followed—different contexts will demand divergent modes of intelligence. In this context, intelligent and even ethical action may seem logically contradictory to those operating at Piaget's **formal level of cognition**. Varela uses the Vajrayana Buddhist tradition's notion of "**crazy wisdom**" to denote someone who has learned to operate at a level of ambiguity and complexity. At another point in his work he refers to such abilities as "intelligent awareness" (Varela, 1999). The critical constructivist teacher and knowledge producer as conceptualized here perform their teaching and research with crazy wisdom and intelligent awareness.

Formal level of cognition constitutes Jean Piaget's highest order of human cognition where individuals exhibit the ability to formulate abstract conclusions, understand cause-effect relationships, and employ the traditional scientific method to explain reality.

Crazy wisdom a concept developed in Vajrayana Buddhism that denotes a form of intelligence that enables an individual to operate at a level of ambiguity and complexity, a form of intelligent awareness that enables improvisational abilities.

In the enactivist frame we crawl outside the conceptual window and move into the post-Cartesian cosmos. In a biological context we come to understand that throughout the world of animals, all beings possess knowledge that is constituted in the concrete situation. I have often marveled at how my dogs, Celtic, Ozzy and Ali, will negotiate a difficult physical maneuver in a way that is cognitively sophisticated and totally improvised within a split-second time frame. In this context we grasp Varela's (1999) point: "what we call general and abstract are aggregates of readiness-for-action" (p. 18). This means that critical constructivist students don't manifest their intelligence simply by developing efficient mental file cabinets for storing data; it tells us that various knowledges are important as we discern their meanings and relationships and become empowered to use them in the improvisation demanded by particular circumstances. In an academic setting the particular circumstance might involve making an argument, defending a position, figuring out how to use knowledge of oppression to help an individual who is suffering, or a teacher knowing how to deal with a student who is having difficulty in a math class.

With this in mind critical constructivists are ready for another cognitive theoretical step forward. Understanding these enactivist concepts concerning the realization of our cognitive abilities in concrete circumstances, we return to the complex dynamics of self-production. In critical constructivism, the understanding of how the self is produced and how this process shapes how we construct the world becomes profoundly important. In modes of teaching and researching where this feature is omitted, nothing can be done to make up for the exclusion. Enactivism refuses to ignore the disjunction between what cognitive psychology has traditionally confirmed vis-a-vis our immediate experience, consciousness or awareness of selfhood. At times in the recent history of cognitive psychology—for example, in behaviorism—scientists insisted that consciousness did not exist because it did not lend itself to empirical measurement. Other cognitive perspectives, while not denying its existence three times before the cock crowed, simply ignored it. Obviously, such approaches to consciousness, immediate experience, and awareness of selfhood left an unfillable theoretical hole in its wake. Why, Varela asks, do humans experience the self so profoundly? Just ignoring the hole will not make it go away.

Critical constructivists ask what is the nature of the disjunction between scientifically validated cognitive theory and our experience of consciousness. Operating on the grounding of our understanding of consciousness construction, we follow Varela's description of the emergent and self-organizing dimensions of selfhood, his notion of the virtual self. The emergent, virtual self arises out of a maze of relationships—in much the same way hermeneutics describes the emergence of meaning in the relationships produced by the hermeneutic circle. It has no definable central processing mechanism, no "brain command" where control is coordinated. Consider this cognitive dynamic in light of our understanding of the cultural politics of the construction of the self. Such a process operates to create new social, cultural, political and economic relationships to produce new and more market-compliant selves. In this context we begin to understand the pedagogical implications of the emergent self. The self is infinitely more malleable, more open to change than we had previously imagined. Given one's motivation, of course, this dimension of selfhood can be mobilized for great benefit or manipulated for great harm.

Critical constructivists enter the arena with a new insight into what can be. They know that despite the power of generations of cognitive determinists operating under the flag of I.Q., human beings can learn to become more intelligent. Individuals can *construct* their own intelligence in a critical constructivist context. And in this context they understand that selfhood is even more of a miraculous phenomenon than many had imagined. In the emergent context we gain a perspective; indeed, to live is to have a point of view. A critical teacher or researcher, however, gains numerous levels of understanding on the origins of his or her perspective. Varela writes of a moment-to-moment monitoring of the nature of our selfhood. Such monitoring involves gaining meta-awareness of the various connections we make to diverse dimensions of the socio-physical world around us. It involves isolating and letting go of an egocentrism that blinds us to the virtual and relational nature of our selfhood. In a critical constructivist context it means avoiding those definitions of higher-order thinking that view it as an egocentric manifestation of the combative proponent of rationality. In the process we also elude the cultural and gender inscriptions such perspectives drag along with them.

From Enactivism to a Critical Ontology: Critical Constructivist Notions of Selfhood

Armed with a critical understanding of self-production and the enactivist appreciation of the emergent self and the power of relationships, critical constructivists move into the realm of ontology. The notion of selfhood and "human being" they pursue is a form of critical ontology. Critical ontology demands that teachers who research the worlds of students, schools and communities also research themselves. In this context teachers explore what it means to be human and to negotiate the social and ideological forces that shape their pedagogical consciousness. In light of a critical knowledge of power, critical constructivists pursue a key dimension of critical ontology—a mode of being that is aware of the ways power shapes us, the ways we see the world, and the ways we perceive our role as teachers and researchers. When teachers possess such understandings, they are better prepared to support or critique what schools are doing and the goals they are promoting. Teachers then become political agents who research their own practices and their own belief systems. In so doing they develop their own teacher personae, not ones that have been insidiously constructed by tacit exposure to the machinations of oppressive power so dominant in the first decade of the twenty-first century.

To gain this literacy of power (Macedo, 1994) teachers must transcend simplistic forms of reflection and move to asking themselves specific questions about whose interests are being served by particular forms of pedagogy and curriculum development. How am I complicit in these political activities? Do I want to contribute to the political agenda being promoted by the existing school organization? Critical constructivist teachers learn that no teaching, curriculum development or knowledge production is value free, no language is politically neutral, and no meaning-making process is objective. They come to understand that the teacher personae they create are committed to something, to the valuing of some politically inscribed educational purpose. Thus, human "being" itself is never a disinterested dynamic and must always be self-monitored for the ways it has been shaped by power.

Thus, a critical ontology pursues human agency—the disposition and capacity to act on the world in ways that involve self-direction and the pursuit of democratic and egalitarian principles of community formation. A critical ontology insists that humans possess inalienable rights to knowledge and insight into knowledge production, to intellectual development, to empowerment, and to political agency in a democratic society. When teachers understand these ontological dynamics and work toward the political goals they portend, they have laid the foundation on which other aspects of professional education can be constructed. They have signaled to those around them that social justice must be integrated into every aspect of education—even the construction of teacher selfhood. With this sense of agency teachers are better prepared to sidestep the technical rationalism and the forces of race, class, gender and sexual oppression that constantly work to shape education in the U.S. (Getzel, 1997; Grimmitt, 1999; Edwards, 2000; Horn, 2000, 2001; Segall, 2002).

Ontological knowledge cannot be separated from experience. Indeed, some might define experience as knowledge translated into action (Ferreira and Alexandre, 2000). Critical ontology is obsessed with new and better ways of being human, being with others, and the creation of environments where mutual growth of individuals is promoted and symbiotic learning relationships are cultivated. Such actions are highly political, involving the knowledge and disposition to escape from technicist modes of social control and knowledge production. The aspect of education that moved me to become a teacher involves this *great escape* and the subsequent move to a new ontological domain. With this in mind we can engage in a form of ontologically catalyzed knowledge production that results in a reconceptualiztion of our lives and, of course, our pedagogy.

Point 6: In this context critical constructivists begin to raise questions about these constructive processes and their relations to power and its influence on the pedagogical processes—informal cultural pedagogy and formal school pedagogy. Here questions of the purposes of schooling in a democratic society begin to emerge.

What are the purposes of schooling in light of the insights of critical constructivism? From my perspective, key purposes of education in a critical constructivist context involve understanding how the present curriculum came to be. In addition, if we understand the forces and assumptions that have operated to shape the existing curriculum, then we need to understand the forces and assumptions that shape our own curricular designs. Thus, to begin with, a key purpose of a critical constructivist education involves understanding that all knowledge is interested—it serves the interests of particular groups in specific ways. What do teachers need to know in order to accomplish such a critical constructivist purpose? What is the critical constructivist teacher's knowledge base? A focus on the way the discipline of psychology has served to position education as a force of social regulation helps us understand the way particular power interests shape the purposes of schooling.

In this context critical constructivist teachers understand that cognition is always a political and ideological act. Indeed, we cannot think about thinking without considering the power dimensions of the act—the empowerment of higher orders of thinking. For critical constructivist teachers to think and operate in this empowered way, they must first get past the notion that thinking is merely an individual psychological activity. As both a psychological and a socio-political activity, complex cognition is in process, ever in a state of being constructed.

For example, teachers are induced by rationalistic management systems to think of the curriculum outside of a social context. In this context political operatives pretend that the knowledges provided teachers and students in expert-produced curricula are politically neutral—a body of agreed-upon knowledge being systematically passed on to students by an ever-evolving, but always neutral, instructional process. Critical constructivist teachers know too much to be seduced by the never-aging sirens of political neutrality. As a deliberate process, the curriculum is always a formal transmission of *particular* aspects of a culture's knowledge. Do we teach women's and African Americans' history in eleventh-grade social studies? Do we read Toni Morrison and Alice Walker in twelfth-grade literature? These are sociopolitical questions—that is, they involve power. The psychological domain involves the same political concepts. The power-related assumptions and practices that characterize contemporary psychology act at a level invisible to many observers. In this way they inscribe the interests of dominant power on the terrain of the cognitive.

Critical constructivist teachers study the subtle ways power inscribes psychology. They are not "conspiracy buffs" who see psychologists as evil villains covertly operating to control the minds of the young and old. Often when discussing the operations of regulatory power, some readers will interpret such analyses of the politics of knowledge and disciplines of knowledge as an effort to uncover conspiracies. While not denying that there are covert actions of power wielders, the analysis of the power of the psychological domain is much less cloak-and-dagger than such a view would imply. Power typically operates here as "common sense," as the unconscious inscription of dominant cultural norms and values onto the nature of psychological knowledge production. For example, by way of its dominant modes of operating, psychology has constructed what we consider the mind to be. The discourse of contemporary psychology has thus created a political reality that, in turn, shapes social organizations, politics in diverse domains, schools, curricula, the role of the teacher and the purpose of education.

Critical constructivist educators maintain that psychology as a discipline that categorizes, classifies and assesses cognition must become more aware of the political consequences of its power to proclaim normality, pathology or a lack of intelligence. Any attempt to reconceptualize contemporary educational purpose must involve tracing the imprint of unexamined sociopolitical assumptions on what psychology presents as objective descriptions of an individual's aptitude. Such pronouncements are ideological as they work to maintain dominant power relations. Far too often it is the socio-economically well-to-do who are deemed intelligent and the poor and racially marginalized who are deemed incapable by the psychological establishment. In this position the critical constructivist educational purpose becomes an act of resistance, a counter-hegemonic struggle to challenge psychological "authority via expertise" (Kincheloe, Steinberg and Gresson, 1996; Bruner, 1996).

Educational psychology as it engages in these processes becomes not a liberating force but a producer of social risks that threaten the well-being of particular individuals. This moves the discipline a long way from the goals of its humanistic origins. The hyperrationality of the positivistic articulation of the discipline with its standardized methods, narrow linear thinking, distance from a naturalistic context and universal application of techniques and assumptions sets up psychology, and the schools it has helped construct, for failure. Because such hyperrationality refuses to consider the sociopolitical role of psychological activities, it produces a bureaucracy of rule-following technocrats. Such functionaries study the mechanical parts of the watch but have never thought about the nature of time. Psychology did not come out of nowhere, but emerged in a particular time and place—the West in the nineteenth century—with particular assumptions and cultural ways of seeing. It has been described many times as a technology of power that affects the lives of different people in diverse ways—some for the better, some for the worse. These dynamics cannot be fully understood outside of social, cultural, political, economic, discursive and even psychoanalytical modes of analysis.

Thus, the cultural inscription on psychology and the ways it contributes to how we conceptualize cognitive activity and the purpose of schooling is palpable. As a creation of power, psychology develops special political relations with particular groups of people. Critical constructivists understand that such exclusions constitute a manifestation of neo-colonial power. Such a colonial power invalidates the cultural production, the cognition and the worth of a vast majority of the people now inhabiting the planet. Critical constructivist teachers cannot stomach such ethnocentric scholarship and in this context work to address such regulatory and exclusionary practices. Many psychologists' pernicious use of African American IQ scores to illustrate black inferiority to whites represents an obvious deployment of psychology as a technology of power. Of course, when such assertions are made, analysts find that tough questions about the nature of intelligence, factors that affect one's relation to the test, the motives of the psychologists involved, or the perspectives of dissenting psychologists are often repressed. Critical constructivists are profoundly interested in these dynamics and what they tell us about the politics of knowledge production and the purposes of schools in contemporary America. They argue that such understandings should be central dimensions of what teachers need to know.

Formulating Educational Purpose: The Critical Constructivist Effort to Resist Regulation

Critical constructivist teachers are "on alert" to the ways Western elitist vantage points are normalized in education. We see them at work in the world of art and art education when dominant power produces accepted modes of representing the world while excluding others (Cary, 1998, 2004). Concurrently, we see such dominant modes of perceiving in history, government, literature and scientific curricula. Students:

- study Western history and views of "others."
- are exposed to little criticism of the structure of the nation's government.
- read the white male canon with a few token additions.
- are shielded from a view of science as a human construction by a particular cultural group at a specific historical time.

We find that the promulgation of such ways of seeing is an attempt to regulate the population, reducing resistance to the interests of dominant groups. Regulated individuals are more likely to accept their places in the workplaces of global capitalism (Kincheloe, 1999). Teachers are not exempt from dominant power's attempts to regulate. Critical constructivist teachers work to expose and confront dominant power's appropriations of what were supposed to be democratic processes. The electronic world of the twenty-first century is vulnerable to power in ways never before imagined. Through not only schooling but by way of television and other modes of communication, dominant power attempts to produce more compliant forms of consciousness and identity. With nearly 24-hour-a-day access to individuals in their most private spaces, dominant power struggles to produce ways of seeing that allow it more freedom to operate (Kincheloe, 2002; Steinberg and Kincheloe, 2004). Both in workplaces and in schools, power wielders offer a debased view of those who they seek to regulate:

- "Incompetent workers" who need to be controlled by top-down management schemes.
- "Unprepared teachers" who need to be provided scripts and planned lessons by experts.
- "Undisciplined students" who are capable of little more than the regurgitation of unconnected facts for standardized tests.

Critical constructivist educators understand that the ways these different groups are represented by dominant power is part of a larger struggle on the landscape of twenty-first century cultural politics and education. If dominant power wins the battle, the oppressive modes of top-down regulation it has devised will be seen as necessary measures to deal with the sea of incompetents that plague our nation. I often listen to individuals speak who parrot the pronouncements of power as mere commonsense: "Somebody's got to do something about all these bad teachers. If they're left to their own devices they'll destroy our children." The cultural struggle over such representations is daunting, as dominant power wielders are the only ones with the financial resources to shape the content of mass media. This makes media literacy (Steinberg, 2004) an extremely important aspect of critical constructivism in general and the rigorous educational curriculum it demands. In this context teachers and their students come to appreciate the politics of knowledge production and information access in the twenty-first century. They understand the inseparability of power and knowledge, the relationship between what dominant power wants us to know and the content of television, radio, movies and school curriculum. Here we can clearly see power's construction of what is considered truth.

These concerns bring us back to critical constructivism's persistent concern with ideology. Dominant power produces ideologies in the contemporary electronic world that appeal to our hearts as well as our minds. The emotional appeal of loyalty to country, for example, despite the ill-advised and violent paths the nation might take, often works as an ideological tool to quell dissent. "I can't speak out against the invasion of Iraq," many assert, "because people will think I'm not a patriotic American." Critical constructivism induces us to embrace civic courage as a central purpose of schooling in a democratic society, to face accusations of disloyalty and to challenge dominant ideological efforts to manipulate public consciousness. The seductions of dominant ideologies are powerful and are by no means easy to resist. Ideologies are the lifeblood of hegemonic power that employs them to win the consent of those being governed to dominant power wielders in government, corporations, and other socio-political locations. Critical constructivist teachers are not afraid to confront these issues.

A central dimension of this confrontation involves questioning that which is typically unquestioned by tracing the socio-historical processes that shaped them. In this act of analyzing how such common-sense achieved its status, critical constructivists begin to understand whose interests are served by such social and educational structures and the ways of seeing they encourage. Such teachers and scholars study the way meaning is shaped in the social, political and educational discourse of the day, in the way cultural signs such as patriotism are deployed in the interests of power. Critical constructivists study the production of such ideology as well as the complex process of its reception. This moves us to a new level of thinking and analyzing, as critical constructivist educators become able to discern hidden meanings and exclusions of political discourse, media production, and school curricula. Through this analysis we become much more insightful about how the socio-political world operates and about our role in it. With such knowledge we are far more capable of resisting the way power works to hurt disempowered individuals, regulate the society, and undermine the democratic purposes of schooling.

Empowered Teachers with a Sense of Purpose

As critical constructivist teachers deploy their abilities to expose the ways school knowledges have been constructed and resist regulation, they become more and more empowered in their efforts to provide an emancipatory curriculum. Indeed, teachers (and their students) are capable of far more sophisticated modes of thinking and analysis than have traditionally been assumed. In this critical constructivist vision, empowered scholar-teachers play a central role in shaping what happens in schools. The role of administrators and educational leaders in this critical constructivist model is to provide room for teachers to operate and support for their professional needs. Central to this support is the creation of a new workplace designed to facilitate teacher scholarly and professional development that is continuing, research based and collaborative. Critical constructivist teacher-educators and educational leaders take seriously the call to provide teachers with an academic preparation that is superior to that offered previously.

Such a critical constructivist teacher education will make sure that teachers possess expert knowledge concerning:

- The nature of student learning
- The scholarly discourses in the liberal arts and sciences
- The practical methods of teaching and classroom management
- The social, cultural, political and economic contexts in which education takes place
- The forms of assessment that promote and appraise higher orders of cognition
- The philosophical understandings integral to the development of a sense of purpose in one's teaching

The only way to guarantee that teachers obtain these knowledges is to cultivate expertise in research. In the best spirit of Deweyan pragmatism, critical constructivist teachers should be able to find answers to questions that arise in teaching via both primary and secondary research. Empowered critical constructivist teachers capable of a life-changing pedagogy need these abilities, need the skills of knowledge production to teach for social transformation and the cultivation of the intellect.

Such empowered teachers no longer need old models of pre-service and in-service training that seek to dictate their work. A critical constructivist teacher education helps teachers cultivate abilities that prepare them to take responsibility for student learning.

Using their skills as knowledge workers, empowered teachers engage students in a mutual process of research and knowledge production that can be used in particular contexts. Thus, scholar-teachers transcend the limitations of positivist visions of education and teaching that de-skill them, take away any need for scholarship, and induce them to ignore the socio-political and cultural dimensions of teachers as knowledge deliverers. Positivist models and the technical standards they support treat teachers disrespectfully and content simplistically.

Advocates of critical constructivism would respect teachers enough to engage them in a conversation about why specific educational reforms would or would not be helpful to them in their professional activities. Such advocates would also open a dialogue about the way such proposals view curriculum content. Questions that would naturally arise in such a conversation would include:

- Is content simply a collection of truths to be passed along to students?
- Is content produced to be questioned?
- What is the teacher's responsibility when confronted by a body of content?
- What are the unstated epistemological assumptions in a body of content?
- What is the relationship of the content to knowledge production?
- Do standards imply a particular relationship between pedagogy and knowledge?
- Does the role of teacher as knowledge worker change the relationship between teachers and content?

If we are serious about improving teacher education and American education in general, we cannot allow epistemologically naïve, top-down, technical standards reforms to disempower teachers and remove them from the educational conversation. It does not seem wise to mandate simplistic, decontextualized content standards and then provide teachers no help in accomplishing them. Critical constructivists understand that this is the worst of all possible worlds. A central feature of a critical constructivist education involves investing in various forms of teacher education that improve teacher scholarship, research ability and pedagogical skills. From classwork in teacher education to research projects to mentoring relationships, teachers must be provided with help in their efforts to develop a new intellectual rigor. None of the talk about educational reform amounts to much if teachers do not assume a new, more scholarly role. In this context teachers and teacher-educators must rethink their own practice, generate new conceptions of student outcomes, and develop engaged pedagogies they have never experienced before. Serious educational reform demands these ambitious reassessments. They will not take place without large-scale social commitment. It is the task of critical constructivists to make a compelling public case for the need for such commitment.

With such public commitments, empowered teachers will have the opportunity to reflect on their skills and pedagogical practices, to engage in research in their subject areas and in the communities surrounding their schools. In such an empowered context, teachers can extend their personal knowledge of students in order to diagnose their academic needs, talents, and personal concerns. In this way more customized and caring experiences can be devised for students, especially those who have been previously ignored in the system. Such reflection, research knowledge and personal insights are then combined with social and pedagogical theoretical knowledge. In this analytical context, empowered teachers formulate their teaching purposes and strategies for attaining them in particular contexts and with specific students.

The Critical Constructivist Teacher Knowledge Base

In this critical democratic framework, teachers take charge of constructing their own pedagogies and educational philosophies. They become detectives of new modes of analysis, new forms of knowledge production and new ways of teaching. A rigorous teacher education grounded on these critical constructivist insights produces educators with a powerful knowledge base:

- Teachers possess an expert knowledge of the liberal arts and sciences, understanding the historical development of disciplines and the various schools of thought within them. Teachers gain a facility to view the discursive aspects of ways of seeing within the disciplines and how these dynamics affect knowledge production within different fields. Weaknesses of the disciplinary arrangement of knowledge are also understood.
- Teachers learn to promote the welfare of their students. Teachers are attuned to students' physical and emotional well-being, as they understand the social and psychological contexts that exert an impact on them. Aware of the importance of making connections with students, teachers develop this ability with students from all backgrounds, dispositions and performance levels.
- Teachers appreciate the complexity of the ways students learn and develop. In this important domain, teachers analyze educational and cognitive psychology and the ways these disciplines interrelate with teaching and the development of educational goals. Understanding the historical and discursive development of the fields of study, teachers explore cognitive activity and learning in a variety of cultural settings. Teachers are cognizant of the constant interaction between psychological assumptions and the way the classroom is organized. A central feature of such studies involves a continuing analysis of human possibility and the development of new cognitive abilities and better ways of being human.
- Teachers both understand students' conceptual development and create ways to facilitate it. A central role of critical constructivist teachers involves identifying the way that students' prior knowledge interacts with academic and other

newly encountered knowledges to shape their view of a specific phenomenon in particular and the learning process in general. Based on these insights, critical constructivist teachers gain the ability to help mediate students' confrontations with the world. Concurrently, such teachers play a hermeneutic role as they help students make sense of and interpret these new encounters in light of their old constructs (Taylor, Fraser and White, 1994).

- Teachers become knowledge workers capable of a variety of research methods depending on the context encountered (Kincheloe and Berry, 2004). Thus, they can produce information and access information to help them better perform their pedagogical tasks. Aware of the politics of knowledge and the changing nature of information production in the twenty-first century, teachers develop interpretive abilities to discern the ways various knowledges are produced, who produced them, and the reason for their production. In the new information order of the twenty-first century, teachers' facility as knowledge workers becomes a basic pedagogical skill. Using such abilities, teachers become aware of the cultural pedagogies produced by television, radio, popular music, the Internet, video games and movies, and their impact on themselves and their students.
- As part of their role as researchers and knowledge workers, teachers study the community surrounding the school for a variety of reasons. In addition to understanding the social and cultural context that immediately surrounds the school, such research enables collaborative efforts with various community members. The integration of school pedagogies with community and institutional expertise is an important aspect of rigorous teacher activity and educational reform.
- Teachers are experts in pedagogical methods and strategies for teaching and classroom management. Teachers learn to use different methods in different contexts and with differing

students with differing needs. Practitioners learn new educational technologies and how they can use such tools to achieve their pedagogical goals.

- Teachers achieve profound expertise in the contextualizing disciplines of education. As they learn about the historical, social, cultural, political, economic, psychological and philosophical contexts that frame education, they develop the important ability to understand the genesis of educational policy and purpose so they can better participate in the public conversation about education. With such skills they are better equipped both to evaluate the curricula and goals they are given and to join the negotiations about such mandates. Such contextual knowledges are central to their self-empowerment.
- Teachers become scholars of education in a democratic society, exploring the ways that an unequal distribution of power and resources insidiously undermines the performance of some students. In this process teachers become scholars of power and justice as they study the complex relationship between educational policy and the pursuit of social justice. In this context teachers understand a variety of manifestations of diversity, analyzing the way race, class, gender, religion, ethnicity and sexuality affect students, teachers and administrators. Cognizant of these effects, teachers are better able to address the problems that emerge when these diversities intersect with the school.
- In light of these expanded abilities and higher expectations, teachers become evaluation experts. As such they develop and utilize a variety of assessment techniques to better understand the impact of their pedagogy. With such knowledge they are better equipped to self-criticize and to monitor student learning so as to continuously update, revise and improve curriculum and instruction. Critical constructivism helps teachers see such evaluation issues as inseparable from their facility as knowledge workers and

researchers. They are simply applying such inquiry skills to what is occurring with their students in their own classrooms.

Critical Constructivism and Informal Out-of-School Pedagogy

Hyperreality
Jean Baudrillard's concept of the contemporary cultural landscape marked by the omnipresence of electronic information. In such a landscape individuals begin to lose touch with the traditional notions of time, community, self and history.

If understanding all of these aspects of the knowledge base were not enough, critical constructivists understand that to create a powerful pedagogy in the twenty-first century they must think of education as something that goes on both inside and outside the school. In the present era of electronic **hyperreality,** critical constructivist educators argue that dominant power's media-based curriculum teaches young and old people alike about the world from a right-wing perspective. A key purpose of any critical constructivist curriculum involves understanding the way regressive ideologies shape both in-school and, especially important now, out-of-school education. In this information-saturated context, it is the duty of critical constructivists to develop methods of studying the cultural pedagogy of hyperreality and its corporate-produced curriculum. Critical teachers carefully monitor and document such a curriculum and its social and political impact. Teachers, educational researchers, political leaders, parents, and students must be empowered to expose the corporate curriculum and to hold corporate decision-makers and their politician allies accountable for the pedagogy they produce.

As critical educators develop methods of analyzing the ideologies of corporate pedagogy as encountered in movies, TV, video games and cyberspace, we must use them to produce a body of information that activists can draw upon. As criticalists gain a more sophisticated view of the ways cultural pedagogy operates, we are better able to expose race, class and gender oppression and even rewrite popular texts when the opportunity presents itself. Critical constructivist analyses can be used to ground strategies of resistance that understand the relationships among cultural pedagogy, the production of knowledge and the construction of subjectivity.

Consider Disney films in relation to the critical constructivist concerns with pedagogy, power, representation and hegemony. Disney films are not the innocent, non-political texts they are structured to appear and assumed to be by liberals and conservatives, filled as they are with implications for economic policy, ecological politics, race, class and gender relations and U.S. domestic and foreign policy. Henry Giroux (1997b) focuses on the gender curriculum of *The Little Mermaid* and *The Lion King*. In both films female characters are depicted within very traditional gender roles, lead lives subservient to men and identify themselves within the parameters of men's positive or negative perceptions of them. In *The Little Mermaid,* Ariel (the young mermaid) in the early part of the film appears to be enveloped in a rebellion against the control of her father in her efforts to pursue a life out of the sea in the world of humans. Soon, however, the audience learns that Ariel trades one form of patriarchal submission for another, as she makes a pact with Ursula, the sea witch, to give up her voice for a pair of legs. The purpose of the deal involves Ariel's desire to engage in a romantic relationship with the handsome Prince Eric.

The cultural curriculum of *The Little Mermaid* teaches profound hegemonic lessons in gender relations: women gain their identity only through the validation of males, and within our patriarchal society women inevitably submit to male authority whether it be that of their father or husband. Thus, such a movie helps shape one's construction of gender roles, including one's own view of self as a man or a woman. Obviously, just because a young woman watches the movie doesn't mean that she will automatically reproduce such gender hierarchies in her life. She may see the movie as we are viewing it here—a text promoting, on one level, patriarchal hegemony. In this context her reading may strengthen her rejection of such ideology. Disney can produce such movie texts, but given the consciousness of particular viewers, they may be received in diverse ways. Even though this is the case, we should never discount the power of dominant hegemonic producers to persuade their audiences of the validity of their representations.

This power is real and frightening in its influence. The **dominant power bloc** uses movie and other media representations to expand its influence, Norm Denzin (1987) argues, by posing as objective depictions of the "real world." Power wielders use film, TV, Internet, CDs, etc. to transmit particular representations. Critical constructivists understand that there is a direct link between cultural representation and hegemonic patriarchal, white supremacist and elite socio-economic class domination. Corporate and business leaders buttress their economic power by using their media access to represent prestige and connect it to the ownership of their products. "Wouldn't you rather drink Beck's Beer, drive an Infiniti, dress in Versace and carried a Gucci bag?" they ask us. The power bloc has the resources to present positive representations of itself to the world. I wrote a book on how McDonald's does just this to create tremendous power and profits around the world (Kincheloe, 2002). Of course, such representations have little if anything to do with any epistemological notion of "truth." They are made-up constructions of reality designed to represent agents of power in ways that are in their self-interest.

Dominant power bloc asserts that power wielders do not constitute a particular class or well-defined social category. The dominant power bloc is more like an ever-shifting set of strategic and tactical social alliances. Such alliances are arranged unsystematically whenever social situations arise that threaten the interests of the "allies."

When we watch TV we see oil and chemical companies representing themselves as champions of environmental protection or automobile companies representing themselves as the homes of happy, contented and empowered line workers turning out products shaped by their highly respected product design input. The **neo-imperialist** or contemporary colonization that the U.S. inflicts on Asian, African and Latin American societies much of the time involves economic and cultural occupation in lieu of military occupation—although with George W. Bush, this is changing. Still, Hollywood and Madison Avenue work hard to represent the world in a way that supports American geopolitical and economic interests (Luke, 1991; Musolf, 1992; Brown, 1993; Kincheloe and Steinberg, 2004).

neo-imperialist Imperialism traditionally involved the process of imposing one nation's power over others by military and political means. Neo-imperialism has relied less on military conquest and direct political rule and more on social, cultural, economic and educational incursions that dominate in more subtle and hegemonic (consent-granting) ways.

Techno-power
as technology, especially information technology, has played a more and more important role in organizing and regulating both economic production and our everyday lives, power has increased in strength and morphed into a techno-power. With important exceptions, technology has been used as a tool of corporate leadership in its attempt to maximize profits and to extend its influence.

Via their ability to use **techno-power** to construct particular representations of the world that support the political, economic and social interests of various elites, diverse power blocs gain unprecedented influence. They are empowered to create, organize, articulate and disarticulate the affective sensibilities and cognitive perceptions that motivate individuals to identify with particular socio-political and educational positions. Simply put, they gain the power to construct consciousness, to shape the ideological perspectives of various individuals. The effort to understand the political realm and the domain of educational politics in twenty-first century Western societies cannot be accomplished outside of an understanding of the power of representation and consciousness construction in previously dismissed cultural and "mere entertainment" venues such as TV, film, popular music, video games, computers and the Internet.

For example, the way whiteness (Kincheloe, Steinberg, Rodriguez and Chennault, 1998) is subtly represented in these cultural domains exerts a major impact on the racial distribution of power. In addition, the way TV erases class relations by portraying contemporary society as classless helps to shape the way wealth is distributed. One is far more likely to see explicit torture and rape scenes and hear the screams of victims than to see representations of the class struggle or hear the world "class." TV news also removes class from contemporary affairs, at most showing brief shots of workers on a picket line during a strike. Doug Kellner (1990) points out that TV news often portrays the strike as a conflict between strikers and consumers, as it focuses its report on how the strike will hurt consumers. Little coverage is given to the unfair corporate policies that motivated workers to take action in the first place (Frankenberg, 1993; Gray, 1995; Bybee, 2004).

In twenty-first century hyperreality, media representations (out-of-school pedagogy) revolving around the axes of race, class and gender play an important role in shaping the nature of Western political-economic, cultural and educational development. These *constructions* of the world are central to this process and are, of course, key concerns to critical constructivists. The ways in which dominant commercial institutions represent blackness are one of the most important stories of our time. These representations and their effects constitute a major concern of criticality. Young black males, for example, have been demonized by conservative-produced media representations designed for airplay in hyperreality.

Young black and often Latino males have been deployed as symbols in the attack on welfare, educational funding, civil rights legislation and job training. Represented in the media as violent and pathological criminals, such young people have been used to rally white racial solidarity and support for racist, right-wing social and educational policies. Using racialized code words to prey upon white fear of young males of color, conservative politicians have tied such young men to the erosion of standards in education and the decline of morality and civility in the public sphere in general. Indeed, the top-down, imposed standards movement of the last dozen years has gained support from these representations. "We've got to impose educational standards before 'these people' destroy our schools," right-wing leaders confide in private. Such constructions work political wonders to create myriad forms of oppression in twenty-first century America. The purposes of critical constructivist pedagogies must take these disconcerting dynamics into account.

Glossary

Assimilation-Accommodation Dyad—To Piaget, intellectual adaptation always involves equilibration between assimilation and accommodation. Assimilation involves the shaping of an event to fit into one's cognitive structure. No event, even if an individual has never encountered it before, constitutes a new beginning. As assimilation fits an experience to the demands of one's logical structures, it is grafted onto previously developed schemes. Accommodation, on the other hand, refers to the restructuring of one's cognitive maps to take care of an event. In order to accommodate, an individual must actively change his or her existing intellectual structure to understand the dissonance produced by the novel demand.

Cartesian-Newtonian-Baconian Modernism —over a period of several decades in the seventeenth and eighteenth centuries, these three thinkers laid the foundation for the western scientific way of viewing the world. Such a mode of understanding would enable scientists to both describe and control the outside world. The foundation established by Carter, Newton, and Bacon allowed science and technology to change the world. Commerce increased; nationalism grew; human labor was measured in terms of productivity; nature was dominated; and European civilization gained the power to conquer in ways previously unimagined.

Crazy wisdom—a concept developed in Vajrayana Buddhism that denotes a form of intelligence that enables an individual to operate at a level of ambiguity and complexity, a form of intelligent awareness that enables improvisational abilities.

Deconstruction—can be defined in many ways—as a method of reading, as an interpretive strategy, and as a philosophical strategy. In critical constructivism it involves all three of these definitions, as it views the world as texts to be decoded, to be explored for unintended meanings. Jacques Derrida has employed deconstruction to question the integrity of texts, meaning that he refuses to accept the authority of traditional, established interpretations of the world.

Dominant power bloc—drawing on theoretical insights from Italian social theorist Antonio Gramsci, British cultural studies scholar Stuart Hall, and cultural theorist John Fiske, the concept asserts that power wielders do not constitute a particular class or well-defined social category. The dominant power bloc is more like an ever-shifting set of strategic and tactical social alliances. Such alliances are arranged unsystematically whenever social situations arise that threaten the interests of the "allies." Dominant power blocs are historically, socially, and issue(s) specific as they come and go in relation to changing cultural arrangements. They are often formed around social arrangements involving race, class, gender or ethnicity in the pursuit of privileged access to particular rights or resources.

Formal level of cognition—constitutes Jean Piaget's highest order of human cognition where individuals exhibit the ability to formulate abstract conclusions, understand cause-effect relationships, and employ the traditional scientific method to explain reality.

Hermeneutic circle—The hermeneutic circle shifts the attention of an analyst back and forth between systems levels, connecting what might seem to some to be unrelated ideas. In the hermeneutic circle the meaning of a phenomenon begins to emerge as parts and wholes are examined in relation to one another.

Hyperreality—Jean Baudrillard's concept of the contemporary cultural landscape marked by the omnipresence of electronic information. In such a landscape individuals begin to lose touch with the traditional notions of time, community, self and history.

Neo-imperialist—Imperialism traditionally involved the process of imposing one nation's power over others by military and political means. Neo-imperialism has relied less on military conquest and direct political rule and more on social, cultural, economic and educational incursions that dominate in more subtle and hegemonic (consent-granting) ways. In such context imperialism attempts to convince the imperialized of its inferiority to and dependence upon the imperializer.

Techno-power—as technology, especially information technology, has played a more and more important role in organizing and regulating both economic production and our everyday lives, power has increased in strength and morphed into a techno-power. With important exceptions, technology has been used as a tool of corporate leadership in its attempt to maximize profits and to extend its influence. Data banks, radio and TV transmissions and transnational communications systems all contribute to a global network that allows corporate leaders to regulate markets and information all over the world. As these communications systems filter into cities, villages and rural areas throughout the world, corporations present ideological views that promote their interests.

CHAPTER THREE

Epistemology, Ontology and Critical Constructivism's Struggle Against Reductionism

Point 7: Critical constructivism illustrates how Cartesian epistemology promotes the notion of the abstract individual—an independent agent free from the constructed influences of the social, political, cultural, economic and historical dimensions of the world. The modernist European concept of self cannot withstand these insights. It is hard in this context to determine where the individual ends and the social begins.

Critical constructivists understand the constructed nature of the world, knowledge and even human beings themselves. A central dimension of critical constructivism and a key dimension of its pedagogy and research agenda involve gaining awareness of ourselves as social, cultural and historical beings. People who gain such an awareness understand how and why their political opinions, religious beliefs, gender roles or racial perspectives have been shaped by dominant perspectives. Critical constructivism is very interested in this construction of self. As critical constructivists expose the particular ways knowledge is produced and the impact it exerts on the production of selfhood, we begin to understand that our present state of being (our ontological self) is, in part, a social and historical construction. Just as the self has been shaped by social action, the self can be rethought and reshaped by social action. In the notion of critical ontology, critical constructivism illustrates the ways the lines between epistemology and ontology are blurred. We are to some degree what we know. As we gain a critical consciousness of this dynamic we can begin to develop new ways of being human.

In this ontological realm, critical constructivism promotes modes of self-analysis that result in changes in attitudes and dispositions. The basis of this change rests on insights into the scars and traumas of the past—one's own and the pasts of others. Critical constructivist teachers working in this context can help their students begin the process of making sense of who they are by bringing to consciousness the process by which their identities were shaped. Action that is to be taken by students to address social pathologies—such as racism, sexism, class bias or homophobia—that shape individual consciousness can begin to be negotiated once self-reflection has taken place. Prudent ontological action that involves asking questions of ethics, morality, politics, emotion and gut feeling does not take the form of rules and precise regulations. Our understanding of critical theory vis-à-vis a complex epistemology provides a framework of principles around which action can be discussed rather than a list of procedures. Teachers who engage in the quest for new, expanded, more just and interconnected ways of being human—a critical ontology—are never certain of the exact path of action they will take in such a pursuit. An awareness of myriad contextual factors will always complicate the effort.

One dimension of the emancipatory action we might take involves questioning accepted definitions of particular social entities such as intelligence, school success, a good society, popularity or competence. As active interpreters with a social/ontological imagination, we can redefine such notions in more just and conceptually expanded ways. In such a context, we can involve ourselves and others in a process of social reconstruction, educational reconceptualization and self-improvement. In a critical ontology grounded on a firm constructivist epistemological set of understandings, individuals hold the power to reconstruct their consciousnesses. If this is the case, then, in a critical ontological context, we possess the ability to reshape ourselves, a process that, given our location in the social web of reality, concurrently demands that we reinterpret our traditions and reinvent our futures together, in solidarity with other self-directed human agents. Here we can see that critical constructivism is not some abstract philosophical position but a way of seeing that holds profound consequences for the way we live our lives and shape who we are.

How we think is profoundly tied to these ontological dynamics. As we understand the various features of critical constructivism, we come to understand both the complexity and limitations of history. Critical teachers not only ask, "How do we know?" but, "Why does it matter to us in this particular place and time?" How does this historical knowledge shape me? What does it demand of me now that I know it? Such questions are central to the reconceptualization of the civic self and the future of democracy in a hyperreal world where power quashes democratic impulses (Pang, Gay and Stanley, 1995). Given such hostile socio-political circumstances, critical democratic educators seek catalysts for ontological evolution. How do we use our critical consciousness to push the boundaries of humanness?

A central step in this process involves freeing ourselves from the machine metaphors of Cartesianism. Critical constructivism recognizes the reductionism of viewing the universe as a well-oiled machine and the human mind as a computer. Such ways of seeing subvert an appreciation of the amazing life force that inhabits both the universe and human beings—a life force that positivism works tirelessly to deny. This machine cosmology has positioned human beings as living in a dead world, a lifeless universe. Ontologically, this Cartesianism has separated individuals from their lifeless surroundings, undermining any organic interconnection of the person to the cosmos. The life-giving complexity of the inseparability of human and world has been lost, and the social study of people has been removed (abstracted) from context. Such a removal has exerted disastrous ontological, psychological and social effects. Human beings, in a sense, lost their sense of belonging to the world and the people around them (O'Sullivan, 1999).

In this context critical constructivism's appreciation of the importance of indigenous knowledge in postmodern times emerges. With the birth of modernism and the scientific revolution, many premodern, indigenous epistemologies, cosmologies and ontologies were lost, ridiculed by European modernists as primitive. While there is great diversity among premodern worldviews, there do seem to be some discernable patterns that distinguish them from modernist perspectives. In addition to developing meaning systems that were connected to cosmological perspectives on the nature of creation, most premodernists saw nature and the world at large as living systems—a viewpoint that in a fascinating way mirrors the psychological-biological theories of the Santiago school of enactivism put forth by Francisco Varela and Humberto Maturana.

Western, often Christian, observers condescendingly labeled such living system perspectives as pantheism or nature worship. In this way they were positioned as an enemy of monotheism, a threat to belief in the true God. As such, they needed to be stamped out and replaced with a belief in Jesus Christ. Not understanding the subtlety and nuance of such indigenous views of the world, Europeans subverted the sense of belonging that accompanied these enchanted views of nature. European Christomodernism transformed the individual from a connected participant in the drama of nature to a detached, objective, depersonalized observer (Semali and Kincheloe, 1999).

The modernist self came out of the Christianization of Europe and the Scientific Revolution alienated and disenchanted. As Edmund O'Sullivan (1999) puts it, Cartesianism tore apart "the relationship between the microcosmos and the macrocosmos" (p. 82). Such a fragmentation resulted in the loss of cosmological significance and the beginning of a snowballing pattern of ontological imbalance. A critical ontology in our critical constructivism involves the process of reconnecting human beings on a variety of levels and in numerous ways to a living social and physical web of reality, to a living cosmos. Educators operating in this conceptual context help students connect to the biotic web of the natural world, the social web of human life, the epistemological web of knowledge production and the civic web of the political domain. In this process they help students connect all of these webs in a manner that provides them the basis of a rigorous, critical education. Students are empowered to make sense of the world and self and the relationships between them. Here critical constructivists move to the realm of critical ontology where new ways of being, and new ways of being connected, reshape all people.

Social psychologist and educator Philip Wexler (2000) picks up on these ontological issues, arguing that an intuitive disenchantment with Cartesian fragmentation and its severing of the self-environment relationship is fueling a diffuse social revaluation. Wexler employs the term "revitalization" for this mass, decentered movement taking place throughout Western societies. It constitutes an attempt, he contends, to resacralize our culture and ourselves. Such an effort exposes the impact of Eurocentrism and Cartesianism on what human beings have become, as, at the same time, it produces an ontological "change from within." Understanding the problems with Cartesianism's lack of self-awareness or concern with consciousness and interconnectedness, Wexler's resacralization picks up on wisdom traditions, both premodern and postmodern, to construct a counter-Cartesian ontology of complexity. In this context, the Cartesian separation of mind and body is repaired, and new relationships and comfort with the body, mind, and spirit are pursued. In the transcendence of modernist notions of bodily ego-greed, a new understanding of the body's role in meaning-making and selfhood is obtained.

Resacralization positions the body in relation to cognition and the process of life itself. The body is a corporeal reflection of the Santiago school's evolutionary concept of **autopoiesis**, the self-organizing or self-making of life. Autopoiesis involves the production of a pattern of life organization. Cognition in this ontological context involves the process of self-*construction*. Thus, life itself is a cognitive activity that involves establishing patterns of living, patterns that become the life force through self-organization. If life is self-organized, then there are profound cognitive, epistemological and ontological implications. Again in this constructivist context we are faced with a profound revelation. By recognizing new patterns and developing new processes, humans exercise much more input into their own evolution than previously imagined. In this context critical constructivism stands at the cusp of a new human journey. In light of these dynamics education becomes an exciting trek in the development of the species in general and individual human beings in particular.

autopoiesis
the self-construction of life forms in interaction with their environments.

Evolution, thus, is not as random as previously thought. Life is self-produced—self-c*onstructed,* in forms of escalating diversity and complexity. The interaction of different living forms can catalyze the self-production feature of living systems. In both its corporeal and cognitive expressions, the autopoietic life process reaches out for difference, for novelty, to embrace its next ontological level (Capra, 1996; Wexler, 2000). Educators who understand these critical ontological dynamics can use them to rethink their lives and their teaching. With these understandings, we can self-organize and reorganize social, cultural, political, psychological and educational scholarship to appreciate new levels of complexity where new patterns and processes allow us to rethink the nature of our being and the possibility of our being. A critical constructivist education in this complex context takes on an unprecedented importance while it pursues ways of knowing and being that shape the evolution of the species. In constructivist terms we pursue epistemologies and ontologies that provide us more power to construct and reconstruct our "selves" in the ways that we want them to be.

Historically Contextualizing the Construction of Selfhood: Critical Ontology Meets Historiography

Thus, I submit this notion of critical ontology with its complex, reflective engagement with the complications of the construction of self and the ways such factors shape teacher selfhood and professional awareness in the twenty-first century. With such dynamics in mind, teachers are asked to confront their ontological relationships with some long-term historical trends rarely discussed in the contemporary public conversation. Critical constructivists maintain these trends hold profound implications for the development of both professional awareness and teacher persona. In my own case, the understanding of my personal historicization in light of five centuries of European colonialism from the fifteenth to the twentieth century—and new forms of economic, cultural, political, military and educational colonialism picking up steam in the contemporary era—is very important knowledge. Indeed, everyone in the contemporary U.S. is shaped by this knowledge in some way whether or not they are conscious of it. We cannot contemplate our professional awareness without reference to these last five hundred and some years and their effects. I was born in 1950, in the middle of the post-colonial rebellion against this half-millennium of colonial violence taking place in Africa, Asia, Latin America and throughout the indigenous world.

While anti-colonial activity continues into the twenty-first century, such discontent reached its apex in the U.S. in the 1960s and early 1970s, finding expression in the civil rights, women's, anti-Vietnam war, gay rights and other liberation movements. By the mid-1970s, a conservative counter-reaction was taking shape with the goals of "recovering" what was perceived to be lost in these movements (Gresson, 1995). Thus, the politics, cultural wars, educational debates, policies and practices of the last three decades cannot be understood outside of these efforts to "recover" white supremacy, patriarchy, class privilege, heterosexual "normality," Christian dominance and the European intellectual canon. I must decide where I stand in relation to such profound yet muffled historical processes. I cannot conceptualize my teacher persona outside of them. They are the defining macro-concerns of our time, as every topic is refracted through their lenses. Any view of education, any curriculum development, any professional education conceived outside of their framework ends up becoming a form of ideological mystification.

The top-down tyranny of expert-produced interpretations of tradition and its oppressive power can be subverted, and our futures can be reinvented along the lines of a critical and complex system of meaning-making. If the right-wing ideological directives of the Bush Administration's Department of Education with their positivistic and duplicitous No Child Left Behind modes of conceptualizing teaching are unchallenged and allowed to prevail, then there is little hope for progressive reform. These issues of self-production will be removed from the consciousness of prospective teachers as they memorize the generic theories and the fragments of the bogus "knowledge base." Relegated to a static state of being, teachers in this technicist paradigm are conceived as a unit of production of an assembly line—historically abstracted selves located outside of a wider social context. Standards reforms that decontextualize teachers and students in this manner are molded by the dynamics of history and social structure (Kincheloe and Weil, 2001).

Identity is never complete and is always subject to modification in relation to prevailing ideologies, discourses and knowledges. A critical constructivist teacher education encourages desocialization via ideological disembedding. Critical complex professional education coursework and practicum experiences focus on the ways in which the values of power-driven, information-saturated hyperreality of the twenty-first century shape the consciousness of both students and teachers (Britzman, 1991; Macedo, 1994; Carson and Sumara, 1997; Soto, 2000, 2001; Apple, 1999; Gordon, 2001; Malewski, 2001a, 2001b). The rigorous study of cultural and historical context alerts prospective teachers to the ways dominant myths, behaviors and language shape their view of the teacher role and the curriculum without conscious filtering. Without this critical constructivist study our ontology is colonized by dominant power. We become beings constructed by others—our actions are manipulated to serve their interests. Critical constructivists deem this to be unacceptable in a democratic society.

The Politics of the Constructed Self: Critical Constructivism, Critical Ontology and Power

Yes, you would be correct to assume that critical constructivism is obsessed by power and its effects. In a critical constructivist context, a critical ontology understands that self-production cannot be understood outside the context of power. Teachers pursuing a critical ontology employ a critical mode of hermeneutics and engage with texts for the purpose of gaining a new level of self-understanding. As previously noted this effort to understand our own social construction is not an invitation to narcissism. Critical constructivists take a shot at Western ethnocentrism. From the critical constructivist perspective education—even, unfortunately, critical education has often contributed to arrogance and narcissism. Critical constructivists operating in the ontological domain pull no punches when they assert that arrogant, egocentric critical scholars insult the critical tradition. Critical constructivism in its awareness of social construction is nothing if not humble. It is humble in its recognition of the magical power of sociopolitical privilege to make one appear intelligent.

In what might be described as the hidden ontology of Cartesianism, students and teachers are not encouraged to confront why they tend to think as they do about themselves, the world around them and their relationship to that world. In other words students and teachers gain little insight into the forces that construct them—that is, that produce their consciousness, shape their subjectivity. In addition, this uncritical articulation of curriculum and pedagogy is virtually unconcerned with the consequences of thinking, as it viewed cognition as a process that takes place in a vacuum. Thinking in a new way always necessitates personal transformation; indeed if enough people think in new ways, social transformation is inevitable.

One reason this situating of self often does not take place in contemporary schooling involves the fact that many of those who teach are denied the historical, philosophical, sociological and cultural studies background to discern what such an act might entail. Insights derived from these domains might have helped teachers figure out the ways that dominant power has subverted democratic impulses in a variety of venues including the political, epistemological, psychological and the curricular and pedagogical. Increasingly dominated by private interests, these domains operated to construct the identities of individuals in ways that were conducive to the needs of dominant power wielders. There were concerted attempts to make individuals more compliant to the needs of corporations, more accepting of government by the market, globalized capitalism, free-market ideologies, the irrelevance of the political domain, etc. The ideological deployment of schools as sorting mechanisms for the new corporate order has gone unchallenged by practitioners unaware of these forces. Where the self fits in these power-driven dynamics is, of course, irrelevant in too many pedagogical venues.

Human efforts to make sense of self and the world are dominated by ideological forces that thwart our pursuit of individual goals. At the same time, particular forms of thinking and action reveal volition and a genuine motivation that transcends the confines of existing social forces—human beings are not pawns of these structures. Social theorists have traditionally been guilty of not recognizing this ambiguity of consciousness construction, identity production and social action. Not until the 1970s and 1980s with the influx of new theories of language analysis and cultural understanding did scholars appreciate the way power was embedded in language and knowledge and the implications of such inscriptions in the production of the self. Human beings are initiated into language communities where women and men share bodies of knowledge, epistemologies and the cognitive styles that accompany them. These are powerful forces in shaping who we are—in constructing the self. Thus, the manner in which we come to think about selfhood and pedagogy is inseparable from these language communities. Indeed, the nature of the curriculum we devise is inseparable from them. A critical ontology understands these dynamics; it understands that the sociohistorical dimensions of self-production are often manifested on the terrain of language.

The schemas that guide a culture and its schooling and help produce subjectivity are too infrequently taught in the hyperrational schools of the twenty-first century. It was the recognition of this same absence in the Italy of the 1920s that social theorist Antonio Gramsci had in mind when he argued that philosophy should be viewed as a form of self-criticism. Gramsci asserted that the starting point for any higher understanding of self involves the consciousness of oneself as a product of sociohistorical forces. A critical philosophy, he wrote, involves the ability of its adherents to criticize the ideological frames that they use to make sense of the world. I watch my colleagues and myself struggle as critical constructivists, as teachers of a complex ontology, as we attempt to engage our students in Gramsci's pedagogical effort to understand themselves in sociohistorical contexts. The work is never easy as many complain and moan about their students' lack of preparation for engagement in such theoretical and introspective analysis. Teachers who engage a complex ontological curriculum must be patient and empathetic with their twenty-first-century students. Our students have very few opportunities in the contemporary world of media- and corporate-influenced schooling to gain experiences that would equip them for such a task.

In very specific terms, a complex ontology is profoundly concerned with the production of self in the context of the influence of power blocs in contemporary society. Such concern reveals itself in a critical questioning of the social, cultural, political, economic, epistemological and linguistic structures that shape human consciousness as well as the historical contexts that gave birth to the structures. Such ontological analysis helps students and teachers explore the sociohistorical and political dimensions of schooling, the kind of meanings that are constructed in classrooms, and how these meanings are translated into student consciousness. Advocates of an ontologically impoverished curriculum often speak of student and teacher empowerment as if it were a simple process that could be served by a $2,000 dollar per day workshop facilitator. "I'm going to make sure you teachers leave here today empowered," the facilitator assures his audience. "Let's make a collage depicting disempowered teachers and one portraying empowered teachers. Empowered teachers are cheerful, they are team players, and they produce the highest student test scores. Let's get to those collages, folks. Be creative, think outside the box." Empowerment is complex and cannot be trivialized like this.

Moving beyond such all too typical trivialization processes, critical constructivists work to construct a rigorous, complex critical curriculum. The question returns: how do we create profound experiences for our students that encourage "ontological makeovers?" Critical teachers must search in as many locations as possible for alternate discourses, for ways of thinking and being that expand the envelopes of possibility. In this context teachers explore literature, history, popular culture and ways of forging community in previously devalued, subjugated knowledges. In this context teachers develop their own and their students' social and aesthetic imaginations. Here we imagine what we might become by recovering and reinterpreting what we once were. The excitement of curriculum as ontological quest is powerful.

Critical Ontology: Reconstructing Ourselves in Interaction with Our Environments

Poststructuralist feminism
a social-theoretical position that questions the universalizing tendencies of structural approaches to scholarship—e.g., Piaget's universal stages of child development or Maslow's hierarchy of needs.

Essentialism
the belief that a set of unchanging properties (essences) delineates the construction of a particular category.

Employing an understanding of complexity theory, Maturana and Varela's Santiago enactivism as the process of life, critical theoretical foundations, the critique of Cartesianism and **poststructuralist feminist** analysis, we can lay the conceptual foundations for a new mode of selfhood. Such a configuration cannot be comprehensively delineated here, but we can begin to build theoretical pathways to get around the Cartesian limitations on the ontological imagination. With Humberto Maturana and Francisco Valera's concept that living things constantly remake themselves in interaction with their environments, our notion of a new self or a critical ontology is grounded on the human ability to use new social contexts and experiences to reformulate subjectivity. In this context the concept of personal ability becomes a de-essentialized cognition of possibility. No **essentialized**, bounded self can access the cognitive potential offered by epiphanies of difference or triggered by an "insignificant" insight.

As we begin to identify previously unperceived patterns in which the self is implicated, the possibility of cognitive change and personal growth is enhanced. As the barriers between mind and multiple contexts are erased, the chance that more expanded forms of "cognitive autopoiesis"—self-constructed modes of higher-order thinking—will emerge is increased. A more textured, thicker sense of self-production and the nature of self and other is constructed in this process. As we examine the self and its relationship to others in cosmological, epistemological, linguistic, social, cultural and political contexts, we gain a clearer sense of our purpose in the world, especially in relation to justice, interconnectedness, and even love. In these activities we move closer to the macro-processes of life and their micro-expressions in everyday life.

A key aspect of the life processes is the understanding of difference that comes from recognition of patterns of interconnectedness. Knowing that an individual from an upper-middle-class European background living in a Virginia suburb will be considered culturally bizarre by a group of tribespeople from the Amazon rainforest is a potentially profound learning experience in the domain of the personal. How is the suburbanite viewed as bizarre? What cultural practices are seen as so unusual? What mannerisms are humorous to the tribespeople? What worldviews are baffling to them? The answers to such questions may shock the suburbanite into reorienting her view of her own "normality." The interaction may induce her to ask questions of the way she is perceived by and the way she perceives others. Such a bracketing of the personal may be quite liberating. This interaction with difference could be another example of Maturana and Valera's **structural coupling** that creates a new relationship with other and with self. In Maturana and Varela's conceptualization, a new inner world is created as a result of such coupling (Maturana and Varela, 1987; Varela, 1999; Sumara, 1996; Sumara and Davis, 1997).

Structural coupling involves recurring interactions that lead to structural interactions between two or more systems. The concept is very important in enactivism and complexity theory in the effort to explain the ways that complex systems develop.

Such explorations on the ontological frontier hold profound educational implications. As critical constructivists pursue rigorous study of diverse global knowledges, they come to understand that the identities of their peer groups and families constitute only a few of the countless historical and cultural ways to be human. As they study their self-production in wider biological, sociological, cultural studies, historical, theological, psychological and countercanonical contexts, they gain insights into their ways of being. As they engage the conflicts that induce diverse knowledge producers to operate in conflicting ways, students become more attuned to the ideological, discursive, and regulatory forces operating in all knowledges. This is not nihilism, as many defenders of the Eurocanon argue; this is the exciting process of exploring the world and the self and their relationship in all of the complexity such study requires. It is the heart and soul of the critical constructivist process—taking charge of the process of our own selfhood, reconstructing ourselves in more just and more intelligent ways.

The process-based and relational notions of self structurally couple with the socio-cultural context and can only be understood by studying them with these dynamics in mind. These characteristics of self hold profound implications politically, psychologically and pedagogically. If our notion of the self emerges in its relationship with multiple dimensions of the world, it is by its nature a participatory entity. Such an interactive dynamic is always in process and thus demands a reconceptualization of the concept of individualism and self-interest (Pickering, 1999). The needs of self and others in this context begin to merge, as the concept of self-reliance takes on new meanings. Notions of educational purpose, evaluation, and curriculum development are transformed when these new conceptions of the personal domain come into the picture. In the first decade of the twenty-first century we stand merely on the threshold of the possibilities this notion of selfhood harbors. The impassioned spirit of critical constructivists is engaged in this moral, intellectual and ontological process.

New Ways of Being, New Ways of Seeing: Critical Constructivism and the Cultivation of the Intellect

Postformal thinking
postformal thinking assumes that there is more to phenomena than initially seems and works to uncover the hidden forces that shape both the phenomena we encounter and the observer's frames of reference.

Central to the goals of critical constructivism's understanding of the social construction of self, and critical ontology's new selfhood, is the quest for different perspectives, new ways of seeing. **Postformal thinking** (see Kincheloe and Steinberg, 1993; Kincheloe, Steinberg and Tippins, 1999; Kincheloe, Steinberg and Hinchey, 1999; Kincheloe, Steinberg and Villaverde, 1999; Kincheloe, 2001, 2004) is important to the development of a critical constructivism with its effort to see the world from as many vantage points as possible. A valuable feature of postformalism's expansion of reason involves the ability to uncover new perspectives, new angles on the world, everyday life and self. In this context students and teachers learn to contextualize in new and exciting ways.

In a postformal classroom, for example, students studying the second US war in Iraq would explore not only U.S. accounts of the conflict but Iraqi perspectives, Islamic perspectives, etc. They would interview gung-ho U.S. Army veterans, opponents of the war, Iraqi victims, and observers from Africa, Latin America and, as Secretary of Defense Donald Rumsfeld puts it, Old Europe. Students would analyze the war in a geopolitical context, a multinational economic context, an environmental context and a medical context. The role of the postformal teacher would involve devising new contexts and new perspectives from which to construct the meaning(s) of the war. Moral and ethical questions would be raised and student interpretations of the event and analysis of its personal meaning in their lives would be encouraged. In the context of critical constructivism, students would study different constructions of the war—not just one "official" construction.

Of course, the efforts of critical constructivist educators pursuing the multiple perspectives of postformalism may often meet with great hostility as proponents of traditional rationality claim that the search for diverse ways of seeing constitutes an assault on reason. In this same critique, many argue that efforts to teach multiple ways of seeing constitute a form of educational indoctrination. The critical democratic education promoted in here demands that students always be allowed to pursue their own conclusions. At the same time many versions of traditional education are guilty of indoctrination by offering students no alternatives to the *truth* of what is being taught. I confidently assert that a student in a critical constructivist classroom will hear more perspectives and have greater freedom of expression than in the scripted classrooms of No Child Left

Behind that are grounded on a narrow one-truth epistemology.

Critical constructivism and postformalism seek to explore that which has been excluded from the validated curriculum. Postformalist pedagogy involves helping students pursue meanings that are often rendered invisible in their taken-for-grantedness in highly regulated standardized classrooms (Mayers and Field, 2004). In curriculum development, an awareness of postformalism's search for difference profoundly shapes the process. Indeed, an understanding of postformal difference helps teachers and educational leaders reflect on school purpose and what it means to be an educated person. Critical constructivists are dedicated to expanding our understanding of difference and its uses in curriculum and in the development of a profound sense of educational purpose (Leonardo, 2004). Since no aspect of society remains unaffected by race, teachers need to listen carefully to, read and interact with those who are racially and culturally different from themselves. The value of the insights about cognition, education, politics and self-construction one picks up in this manner are invaluable to personal and social growth.

New ways of seeing help teachers and students achieve higher levels of self-awareness. Empowerment within this context involves the development of minds liberated from stale convention, a critical consciousness and a free society. Critical postformalist teachers who can see from a variety of often forbidden perspectives become aware of the construction of their own professional consciousness and the ways that social and institutional forces work to undermine their autonomy as educators. As critical constructivism positions the teacher self "in question," self-images, inherited dogmas and absolute beliefs are called into question. Critical teachers in this process begin to see themselves in relation to the world around them, to perceive the school as a piece of a larger mosaic. Teachers begin to see an inseparable relationship between thinking and acting, as the boundary between feeling and logic begins to fade from the cognitive map—a map redrawn by postformalist multiple ways of seeing.

To value different ways of seeing is on some level to acknowledge the interconnectedness of human beings and to reject the isolated, abstract, logical individual of Cartesianism. Critical constructivism breathes pedagogical life into this concept as it accounts for the human environment, the lived worlds of students and teachers and the larger social contexts in which schools operate (Teitelbaum, 2004). This emphasis on difference, biography and social context moves students to the ontological concern of how we evolve and develop new ways of being human. Taking its cue from our theoretical bricolage, especially enactivism, critical constructivism views the connection with difference as central to human evolution.

Here we connect the epistemological domain of gaining and enacting knowledge to the ontological realm of who we are in relation to this process of learning. With this in mind, critical constructivists pay close attention to the conditions in which humans confront knowledges, learn, grow and develop. Obviously, these conditions are socially constructed as is the language used in them. Individuals, no matter how brilliant, can't create the conditions in which they learn and develop. Thus, our social interconnectedness is pre-given. As we grow and develop, we gain the ability to choose to some extent how to extend and nurture the interconnections we make. We can avoid the exclusions that race, class, gender, sexuality, geographical place and religion often create for us. In this context we can ignore the socio-cultural "no trespassing" signs that segregate us from one another. Critical constructivists transgress established norms as they move into "dangerous" domains.

Francisco Varela (1999) describes this ontological dynamic as he discusses the nature of the relationship between self and environment. Everyday life, he asserts, can be described as the domain of situated agents continuously dealing with unexpected events. They cannot devise some master plan to lead them step by step through the wilderness. They must develop the wisdom and reflective ability to respond to the ill-defined and contextually specific conditions they encounter. In this individuals can either embrace and expand their interactions, or they can retreat and limit such connections. Critical constructivists and postformalists thirst for new interactions and connections. They see themselves as cognitive adventurers who get a "rush" from the process of exploring new ways of seeing. As teachers, they can hardly wait to get to their classrooms to help their students gain the excitement and insight that come from this process. It is in this embrace that they expand the domain of education and selfhood.

Critical Constructivism and the Contemporary Alienated Self: Critical Ontology and Human Possibility

In a critical ontological context, curriculum development and the learning processes become profoundly exciting enterprises because they are always conceptualized in terms of what we can become—both in an individual and a collective context. In our socio-ontological imagination we can transcend the Enlightenment category of abstract individualism and move toward a more textured concept of the relational individual. Indeed, critical constructivists argue, we can reconstruct the species. While abstract individualism and a self-sufficient ontology seem almost *natural* in the Western modernist world, such is not the case in many non-Western cultures and has not been the case even in Western societies in previous eras. In ancient Greece, for example, it is hard to find language that identified "the self" or "I"—such descriptions were not commonly used because the individual was viewed as a part of a collective who could not function independently of the larger social group (Allen, 2000). In the "commonsense" of contemporary Western society and its unexamined ontological assumptions, this way of seeing self is hard to fathom.

The Cartesian ontology of the European

Enlightenment (beginning around 1650) discerns the natural state of the individual as solitary. The social order in this modernist Eurocentric context is grounded on a set of contractual transactions among isolated individual atoms. In other works I (Kincheloe, 1993) have referred to Clint Eastwood's "man with no name" cinematic character who didn't need a "damn thing from nobody" as the ideal Western male way of being—the ontological norm. Operating in this context, we clearly discern, for example, cognitive psychology's tradition of focusing on the autonomous development of the individual. Critical constructivist psychology produces a conception of mind not as a solitary information processor but as a system that connects the human brain to the tools and symbol systems employed in social interaction.

Thus, the higher cognitive functions of human beings are always socially and culturally mediated by language and other tools (Dougiamas, 2002). In the critical constructivist and critical ontological contexts, a human being simply can't exist outside the inscription of community with its processes of relationship, differentiation, interaction and subjectivity. Indeed, in this critical ontology, the relational embeddedness of self is so context dependent that psychologists, sociologists and educators can never isolate a finalized, completed "true self." Since the self is always in context and in process, no final delineation of a notion such as ability can be determined. Thus, we are released from the rugged cross of I.Q. and such hurtful and primitive conceptions of "intelligence." With advocates such as Jerome Bruner (1996), Ernst von Glaserfeld (1980, 1993) and Humberto Maturana and Francisco Varela (1980, 1987), constructivist concepts in psychology have been more and more accepted.

One can quickly discern the political consequences of such a Cartesian ontology. Human beings in Western liberal political thought become abstract bearers of particular civic rights. If individuals are relational, context-embedded beings, however, these abstract rights may be of little consequence. A critical ontology insists that individuals live in specific places with particular types of relationships that play a central role in the construction of the self. They operate or are placed in the web of reality at various points of race, class, gender, sexual, religious, physical ability, geographical place and other continua. Where individuals find themselves in this complex web holds dramatic power consequences. Their location shapes their relationship to dominant culture and the psychological and curricular assumptions that accompany it. In other words, the intelligence mainstream psychology deems these individuals to possess profoundly depends on this contextual, power-inscribed placement. A prime manifestation of ontological alienation involves a lack of recognition of the dramatic effect of these dynamics on everything that takes place in the psycho-educational cosmos.

In the context of our critical ontology, the autonomous self with a fixed intellectual ability becomes an anachronism. As an effort to appreciate the power of human beings to affect their own destinies, to exercise human agency and to change social conditions, critical ontologists study selfhood in light of the sociological, cultural studies, cultural psychological and critical analytical work of the last few decades. Much of what dominant psychology and education consider free will and expressions of innate intelligence are simply manifestations of the effects of particular social, cultural, political and economic forces. While we can make decisions on how we operate as human beings, they are never completely independent of these structuring forces. This is true whether we are Diane Ravitch or Michel Foucault—neither person can operate outside of society or free from cultural, linguistic or ideological influences.

It is important to note here that neo-positivist educational policy makers of the twenty-first century contend that their work takes place outside of the influence of these dynamics. They claim that their work avoids cultural values and morally inscribed issues, and because of such diligence, they have presented us the truth about how students learn and how teachers should teach. In the critical ontological context developed here, such researchers must take a closer look at who they are and the structuring forces that have constructed their views of the world, mind and self. Their inability to discern the effects of these forces reflects the ontological alienation referenced here. Such alienation undermines their ability to imagine new and better ways of being human both for themselves and for the teachers and students their knowledges and policies oppress. Critical constructivism offers a way out of this unproductive situation.

Point 8: Critical constructivists avoid reductionism and the naïve realism that accompanies it. Critical constructivist educators make sure that education does not serve as a force that indoctrinates and stupidifies rather than engages and enlightens.

One of the most basic assumptions embedded in contemporary reforms and the technical standards that accompany them is that the world is a simple system made up of entities capable of precise empirical description. Such a way of viewing knowledge allows teachers, educational leaders, curriculum developers and students to run away from complexity and hide in a shelter of mediocrity. Such a low-level thinking undermines the social order on a multitude of levels and weakens civic and democratic structures. Such naïve realism promotes a view of knowledge-production where ancient Greek notions of "gaining insight" are replaced by an obsession with following the "correct" method. Here knowledge production is *reduced* to a notion of rigor that relies exclusively on fidelity to the scientific method. Thus, knowledge production is no longer an act of insight, contextual analysis, intuition and creative brilliance as much as it is a *procedure*. Critical constructivists demand something more.

Viewed as a procedure, knowledge production turns away from concern with the multiple relationships between entities, the larger processes of which they are a part, the new understandings to be gleaned from examining the same thing within different contexts. Instead, realist knowledge producers focus on understanding the objective world and its contents as isolated entities, things-in-themselves. In this epistemological framework these things-in-themselves wait around for a knower to arrive and "discover" them by using the right procedure. Such a way of perceiving shapes not only knowledge production but knowledge reception as well. Assumed in the realist scheme is the belief that knowledge discovery is the end of the process—after we "know" one of these things-in-themselves, there is nothing more to learn. Thus, the purpose of schooling grounded on this construct is simply to obtain the knowledge already produced—a.k.a., the truth.

Critical constructivists talk about analysis, interpretation, complexity, relationship, insight, creativity or higher-order thinking is a waste of time in the context of naïve realism. The work has already been done, and the knowledge has been produced by the experts. Teachers in this reductionistic context simply induce students to commit the truth to their memory banks. This is one aspect of the logic that serves to dumb down teacher education and public education at the beginning of the twenty-first century. In philosophical language, this influential concept of thing-in-itself has been referred to by its detractors in the Western tradition as the category of substance. In this disciplinary lexicon, substance implies that what we know has a material quality, it is *something*. The traditional dissenting viewpoint asserts that what is ultimately important in worldly affairs is immaterial, is the *no-thingness* of relationships and connections between things. A relationship or a conceptual connection can many times not be expressed in an empirical manner. From the naïve realist perspective, this renders it irrelevant.

Realist truth claims are riddled with problems as the aforementioned issues contributing to educational complexity are ignored. The content realist methods produce is not the neutral result of objective procedures as it is portrayed. A plethora of value choices and subjective judgments have gone into the production of the final product of inquiry. This final product (data) is the result of a procedure-driven chronicling of the decontextualized thing-in-itself. Such a removal from the various contexts that shape its meaning render such "validated knowledge" less trustworthy than scholars and teachers have traditionally assumed. Andrew Murphie (1998) labels knowledge produced by more contextualized and complex methods "objectiles." An objectile escapes this realist thing-in-itself reductionism and simplification and comes to be defined by its movement and change and its connections with other objectiles. The researcher, knowledge analyst, teacher, and learner can use the insights gained from the notion of the objectile to become far more sophisticated knowledge workers and thinkers. They understand that objects in both the physical and social worlds are not merely solid and independent entities. Instead, critical constructivist learning that recognizes complexity is more concerned with an object's connections to other objects than its substance.

There are numerous examples of the importance of connection in the world around us. Art has always had objectile properties as the positioning of images in relation to one another is seen as more important than the isolated image. In contemporary electronic reality, hypertext with its series of links from one site to another illustrates connectivity well. In hypertextuality the site possesses no presence that transcends its reference to somewhere else. In this cyber-context, connection and relationship take on a new importance as we construct various Web sites and seek knowledge on those already created. Understanding the influence of connection and relationship in the construction of knowledge, critical constructivists grow even more aware of the fallibility of researchers and so-called experts. As construct theorist and ancestor of constructivism George Kelly (1955) argued, all existing interpretations of social and physical phenomena are subject to rethinking and revision (Chiari and Nuzzo, 1993). In the context of connection and relationship we can extend Kelly's idea in light of our understanding that one's view of any "thing" will change when we see it in connection to a new phenomenon or in a new relationship. In this context critical constructivists understand that new ways of seeing the phenomena of the world and the world itself are always subject to change.

Avoiding Technicalization and Simplification

What we label knowledge, the ways it is arranged and presented, the ways it is taught and learned and what is considered an appropriate display of having learned it, are inseparable from the way we view the world, the purposes of education, the nature of good society and the workings of the human mind. Such issues are connected to issues of power and questions of who is entitled to promote their view of the world. Thus, the contemporary effort to hold educators accountable is not some simple process where experts simply decree the correct instrument to measure the process. Instead, it is part of a larger struggle between proponents of various worldviews, social visions, and conceptions of what it means to be human. Critical constructivists maintain that in order to contribute to the effort to improve education, teachers, students, parents, politicians and community members must gain a more textured understanding of just what is being discussed here.

The worldview and epistemology that support educational standardization assume that absolute forms of measurement can be applied to human endeavors such as education. The teaching and learning processes, advocates of technical standards believe, are sufficiently consistent and stable to allow for precise measurability. The strategies that educators use and the factors that produce good and bad student performance can be isolated and even expressed in mathematical terms. Therefore, questions based on students' acquisition of selected bits of knowledge can be easily devised, and we can determine a student's and a teacher's competence with little difficulty because such measurements can be accurately made; advocates of technical standards see little trouble holding teachers accountable. Critical constructivists want to move beyond this simplified model to help all parties understand the multiple contexts that shape in diverse and sometimes conflicting ways what is going on in such a process. Despite the pronouncements of many experts, the evaluation process is more complicated than simply designating the mastery of a fragment of content as an objective and then determining if it has been achieved.

But reductionistic ways of seeing continue to hold sway in the public conversation about educational reform. One reason for this may involve the simplification process referenced here—they are easy for everyone to understand. Simplicity sells; complexity doesn't. "We can keep close tabs on student performance at the school level," advocates of reductionism tell the public. "Using our mathematical measurement of student acquisition of content," they continue, "we can compare the performance of schools, school districts, states and nations regardless of the contextual differences that make them unique." All of these measurements and comparisons are guided by a *faith* in the value of standardized content-based tests. The faith in the meaning of what is measured by such tests is not grounded in some form of rigorous empirical evaluation.

The idea that such tests measure student achievement or ability and teacher effectiveness is a construction, an interpretation—nothing more, nothing less. Obviously, critical constructivists have no trouble with interpretations—all knowledge is produced by an interpretive process. The problem here is that advocates of reductionism and the standardization of education do not reveal the interpretive aspects of the testing process; they present the data and its meaning as scientifically validated truth. A rigorous analysis of how such truth is constructed reveals many interpretive (subjective) steps in the process. Critical constructivists insist that the justifications for particular interpretations of test meaning be provided and claims of objectivity in such an accountability process be abandoned.

Guided by a leap of faith in what tests tell us about

the educational process, naïve realists, reductionists and advocates of technical standards have unleashed a process where students and teachers will be ranked and ordered to an unprecedented degree. Once students are placed in the low rankings, it becomes extremely difficult to get them out. Thus, technical standards advocates, along with the testing and the ranking that accompany these standards, are willing to construct an entire educational system including its purposes and rewards and punishment structures on a faith in the worthiness of an unexamined standards production and standardized testing process. In the norm-referenced measurements used in this context, there must be winners and losers.

The fact that there are losers "proves" the system's rigor. Students are pitted against one another in a fierce competition for restricted rewards. As teaching and learning are reduced to knowing *what,* meaning is lost. Tragically, particular patterns begin to emerge involving which demographic groups tend to succeed when schools are arranged in this manner. Often students who come from lower socioeconomic and non-white families do not have the benefit of a parent who has a college degree. In homes where parents perform low-skill jobs, families may not see schoolwork as as important as do families of upper-middle class, white, English-speaking students. Studies of the social context of schooling point out that poor and racially marginalized students have learned to view academic work and the testing of technical standards as unreal, as a series of short-term tasks rather than activities with long-term significance for their lives.

Without such compensation or long-term justifications, such students may display little interest in academic work. Their poor performance on the tests and subsequent low ranking are viewed in the context of objectivist technical standards as a lack of ability and academic failure. Their faith in the testing process moves them to issue a scientifically validated assessment of "cognitive inferiority" to such students. Such a decontextualized, reductionistic view of the complex process of schooling and student performance is unacceptable—indeed, it is socially dangerous as it contributes to an unfair, unjustifiable sorting of the haves and the have-nots. Teaching is simplified; teachers are deskilled, and students who fall outside particular "mainstream" demographics are severely punished. Even students from the mainstream are subjected to an inferior, simplified education despite the fact that many of them may succeed in the system of rewards. In such a reductionistic system their scholarly abilities are undermined and their view of themselves and the world obstructed. Their understanding of the ways knowledge and selfhood are constructed is eclipsed. Critical constructivism takes on an urgent importance in this social context, as it attempts to rectify the human damage caused by technical reductionism.

Reductionism and Stupidification

Objectivist views of the world have been trapped by the mindset that locates truth in external reality—there is no need for constructivism in this epistemology. Curriculum in the educational institutions that emerge from this philosophical position become little more than an effort to accurately reflect this reality in a way that avoids challenging the status quo. Indeed, Cartesian reductionism represents thought as simply an inner process conducted in the minds of autonomous individuals. The thoughts, moods and sensations of these individuals are separate from their histories and social contexts. If thinking and curriculum development are to be seen as simply mirroring external realities, then there is no need for philosophy in general or critical constructivism in particular.

From the reductionistic perspective, the ability to conceptualize or to engage students with the complexity of knowledge work has little to do with culture, power or discourse, or the tacit understanding unconsciously constructed by them. More philosophically oriented observers may contend that this is a naïve view, but the naïvete is recognizable only if knowledge construction is understood as a multidimensional and ambiguous social activity. Mind is more than a repository of signifieds, a mirror of nature. As previously maintained, critical constructivism assumes that the mind constructs rather than reflects, and the nature of this construction cannot be separated from the surrounding social world.

Objectivism undermines the most creative dimension of living organisms, of the human being in particular—the ability to not merely respond to the environment but to construct meaning about it, to represent it in a variety of ways. Of course, this is not an objective process but a highly subjective one. The observer is not independent from this process as objectivism and reductionism would have it but intimately engaged. The process of constructing knowledge is inseparable from the conceptual frameworks, cultural assumptions and epistemological structures in which the human agent operates. As Maturana and Varela argue, humans bring forth perspectives on the world based on what they see as a unity—a constellation of connections among phenomena. This bringing forth is an act of autopoiesis—self-construction. Self-construction whether of one's selfhood or of knowledge is a cognitive act. It is the act that all living things engage in. It is ironic that objectivism attempts to undermine an action so central to being alive. Critical constructivism wants to return the sanctity of autopoiesis to the scholarly act, to pedagogy (Chiari and Nuzzo, 1993; Matthews, 2003).

Critical constructivists always keep these autopoietic notions in mind. As they build a curriculum, they are acutely aware that knowledge emerges neither from subjects nor from objects but from an interactive relationship between the knower (subject) and the known (object). Drawing from Jean Piaget, this relationship is represented by the assimilation-accommodation dyad. Employing these conceptualizations, teachers operating in the zone of constructivism conceive knowledge as culturally produced and recognize the need to construct their own criteria for evaluating its quality. This critical constructivist sense-making process is a means by which teachers can explain and introduce students to the social and physical world and help them build for themselves an epistemological and ideological infrastructure for interpreting the phenomena they confront and for constructing knowledge.

Here rests a key dimension of critical constructivism and the pedagogy it supports. Such teachers realize that because of the social construction of knowledge, their interpretations and infrastructures are a part of the cosmos but are not simply a reflection of the cosmos. As a result, the curriculum they develop is self-consciously fallible and unafraid to highlight the mistakes made by curriculum developers operating in its name. This process of understanding the nature of pedagogy and curriculum, its all-important relationship to the individual's act of learning and its metaperspective on its relation to the world, is a key feature of a critical constructivist education. It is by gaining these insights that we begin to escape the stupidification of the reductionistic view of knowledge and the rote learning of information fragments of the standardized content-standards curriculum of the twenty-first century (Benson, 1989; Bowers and Flinders, 1990; Knobel, 1999; Denzin and Lincoln, 2000).

In the contemporary era we all know the reductionistic curriculum story: in the name of efficiency, we identify the specific body of information to be learned and the "proven" methods of teaching and learning it. Such a positivistic bedtime story forces us to accept without question that the specific body of knowledge to be learned is valid, that it belongs in our classrooms. Teachers and educational researchers need not trouble themselves with inquiry about the ideological interests of this knowledge. Educational researchers need concern themselves only with empirical investigations of how best to teach this information—how to insert it into the minds of students so it can raise test scores. If we manipulate this variable in this specific way, do students acquire more or less of the knowledge? Thus, many would argue, educational issues in this positivistic framework are reduced to technical issues.

Questions of ends or purposes are subservient to questions of means or techniques. Critical scholars have labeled this tendency "instrumental rationality." Advocates of critical constructivist approaches to educational research (Kincheloe, 2003) argue that the purpose of educational activity must always be an integral aspect of the research process.

When researchers separate purpose from educational research, the tendency to break learning into discrete pieces considered in isolation is perpetuated. In the instrumental rationality of James Mill's "mental mechanics," through Edward Tichener's structuralism, to behavioral objectives and componential objectives, and now to technical standards, reductionistic educators have assumed that the whole was never more than merely the sum of the parts. Houses from this perspectives are no more than the nails and lumber that go into them, and education is not more than the average number of objectives mastered. Many educators have referred to this fragmentation process as "bitting." It is not hard to imagine a curriculum caught in the bitting process. Students copy information from chalkboards and overhead projectors and skim textbooks to find information fragments that would answer the question both in the standards study guides and on the multiple-choice tests.

Children listen (when they're not talking); they respond when called upon; they read fragments of the textbook, and they write short responses to questions provided on worksheets. They rarely plan or initiate anything of length or conceptualize their own projects. They rarely even write essays. They are learning to be deskilled, to be passive, to be citizens who are governed, not citizens who govern. They are learning not to construct their worlds but to have their worlds constructed for them. They are taught not to seek deep structures that move events but to examine only the surface level of appearance. They will not understand the process of consciousness construction or the subtlety of the process of hegemony. Ideology will remain an incomprehensible abstraction in their eyes—they will be stupidified, as Donaldo

Macedo (1994) puts it. Those students who will transcend such blindnesses will make their emancipatory journey despite their classroom experiences, finding analytical inspiration oftentimes outside the school context. The reductionistic, technical-standards-driven curriculum serves to perpetuate the most pernicious effects of bureaucratized school practices (Bracy, 1987; Ohanian, 1999; Horn and Kincheloe, 2001).

Just as objectivist standards present an authoritarian view of how curriculum development should take place, they also shape how teachers relate to expert-produced knowledge about education. In the context created by reductionistic technical standards, we know that experts produce pedagogies that are applied to achieve the goal of higher standardized-test scores. Such reductionistic "expertise" sets up a context where the factory-model division of labor is reproduced: the expert conceptualizes the teaching act and produces theory; the practitioner executes the directives of the official data. The teacher is alerted to some weak component of his or her pedagogy by the expert's comparison of it to a research-grounded scientific theory. The expert then provides the teacher with a choice of scientifically validated teaching strategies. The teacher exercises his or her professional autonomy, selecting, applying and then practicing a strategy in a supervised training session where contextual variables have been controlled. The result is a scientific curriculum that efficiently teaches the official factoids.

All phases of such a reductionistic process depend on an instrumentally rational concern with the measurable results of particular strategies. Does the strategy serve to raise standards-driven test scores? No questions are asked about issues such as the worth of raising the scores, the tacit view of intelligence embedded in them, or the educational and political side effects of viewing their improvement as the primary goal of teaching. Value dimension and ideological dimensions of human practice escape the vision of this authoritarian reductionism. No room for uncertainty or spontaneous innovation exists;

teachers and students lose their ability to shape the curriculum in light of their needs and local conditions. Education research on the part of the experts is reduced to the attempt to find relationships between specific teaching skills and test score improvement. We make "remarkable" findings that are passed along to teachers and teacher-education students—for example, the more time students study a particular subject, the greater the possibility that they will raise their test scores in that subject. Such a reductionistic **logocentrism** forces us to focus on the least-important aspects of curriculum development, aspects that are inevitably the most measurable (Eisner, 1984; Schon, 1987; Kroath, 1989; Pinar, 1994).

Logocentrism an embrace of reason accompanied by the exclusion of the affective, the emotional aspects of learning and knowing and the cultural context in which it takes place.

The reductionistic logic of the stupidified, objectivist curriculum attempts to train teachers to place their faith in a rationalized curriculum of pretests, drill work and posttests. Such an orientation tames the pedagogical imagination and drenches the impassioned spirit, as critical constructivist teachers find that they are increasingly viewed as troublemakers and malcontents. In the reductionistic logic of top-down technical standards, teachers are *conditioned* to internalize as common sense a professional approach that breaks the complex task of teaching into a series of simple steps that even unskilled laborers can perform—that is, they have been *deskilled.* As efficiency expert Frederick Taylor put it to one of his workers: "You're not supposed to think; there are other people paid for thinking around here" (quoted in Wirth, 1983, p. 12). The need for the judgment of the worker would be eliminated in Taylor's efficient system. The devisers of technical standards learned Taylor's scientific management lessons well. Using the standardized technical controls of technical standards, teaching and curriculum development are rationalized; the conception of the pedagogical act is separated from its execution.

In this reductionistic curriculum teachers do not need to learn the intricacies of subject matter, nor do they need to understand the socio-historical context in which the knowledge to be taught was produced. All they need to do is take the content of the standards, break it into components, present it to the student, and test him or her on it. How can those critical constructivist malcontents argue with this process? It is a pedagogy as right as rain, so commonsensical it defies the need for justification. Why would we need teachers to be scholars, curriculum developers, or knowledge workers in this technical-standards-driven context? Obviously, we don't—well-educated teachers, a rigorous teacher education, and practitioners capable of producing research about their communities, schools and students are all irrelevant in the deskilled content of top-down technical standards. Critical constructivists envision a different world, a different pedagogy and a different purpose for education than do the advocates of technical standards.

Critical Constructivism and the Effort to Overcome Reductionism and Its Fragmented Curriculum

Naïve realism and the reductionistic curriculum it supports have fragmented the world to the point that individuals are blinded to certain forms of human experience. Attempting to study the world in isolation, bit by bit, education scientists have separated the study of schools from society. For the purpose of simplifying the process of analysis, disciplines of study are divided arbitrarily without regard for larger context. In this mode of thinking, technical standards have been formulated outside of wider cultural and political concerns for empathy. Without these dynamics, difference is often read as deficiency, if not pathology. This holds not only cognitive implications but social, cultural and political ones as well. As politicians mandate technical standards and test-driven curricula, they extend these problems and create an exaggerated form of cognitive reductionism. Finding its roots in this modernist fragmentation, the reductionist curriculum exacerbates the "factoid syndrome" where students learn isolated bits and pieces of information for multiple-choice tests.

Within this concept rests a central critique issued

by critical constructivists: the cognitive reductionism of the objectivist curriculum fragments meaning as it fragments information. In this curricular context, the relationships that connect information about the world and provide meaning to human observers are dismissed from consideration. Objectivism and the education it promotes undermine the complexity of the knowledge production process. The very features of the world that help us construct meaning about it are undermined by the rationalized and fragmented curriculum. Understanding these relationships and applying such insights to the effort to construct a better world should form the foundation of the curriculum. At the very least, they should not be ignored. To dismiss such dynamics in the shaping of the curriculum is a form of irrationality that operates in the guise of rationality. This concept is not hard to understand, and once the public appreciates it, educational reform will never take place in the same way again.

The cognitive reductionism and the modernist fragmentation such irrationality produces have weakened our ability to see the relationships between our personal actions and the cosmos, our social constructions and the world around us. As reductionists come to value autonomy over participation, isolation over communion, they begin to view natural phenomena as objects for exploitation and manipulation. Science thus mutates into a device for prediction and control that is comfortable when, in the name of progress and short-term profits, it leads to a rape of the natural world (Rifkin, 1989; O'Sullivan, 1999). Thus, the fragmentation of information and meaning and the cognitive reductionism of technical standards produce reverberating consequences throughout the social world. What critical constructivists are analyzing here involves the often-hidden organizing principles upon which a society constructs itself and its future. Thus, these ideas are central not only to education but also to who we are as inhabitants of the planet.

Reductionism's unquestioning educational trek for absolutism and certainty results in a twelve- to sixteen-year training program for Cartesian-Newtonian modernity. Modernist technicist curricula emphasize quantities, distance and location, not qualities, relationships or context. Modernist reductionistic assumptions are deeply embedded in various aspects of school life. The tests typically given in reductionistic schools, for example, prepare students to think in terms of linear causality and quantification—the foundations of modernist reductionism. Because we are not taught to think in complex constructivist terms, in terms of exposing the tacit assumptions embedded in our conventions and everyday practices, disempowered teachers are oblivious to the fact that they are propagating a specific ideology when they design their curricula and administer the standards-driven "objective" tests.

Objectivist education is chained to a bed covered with a crazy quilt of unexamined assumptions. These hidden assumptions dictate the questions asked about schooling in the public conversation and the tenets of the reform proposals offered by politicians. They play a powerful role in the way individuals in contemporary society construct their view of public schooling and what it should be doing. Reductionists attempt to piece Humpty-Dumpty back together again by employing more and more of the king's horses and men—they attempt to reform schools with only our existing tools. They think of schools in the context of the objectivist assumptions, refusing to realize that the educational crisis of the twenty-first century is symptomatic of the larger enigmas of modernist fragmentation.

Glossary

Autopoiesis—the self-construction of life forms in interaction with their environments.

Essentialism—the belief that a set of unchanging properties (essences) delineates the construction of a particular category.

Logocentrism—an embrace of reason accompanied by the exclusion of the affective, the emotional aspects of learning and knowing and the cultural context in which it takes place.

Postformal thinking—emerging from postformalism, postformal thinking moves beyond Jean Piaget's notion of formal thinking as the highest order of human thinking. Challenging Cartesian-Newtonian forms of cognition, postformal thinking assumes that there is more to phenomena than initially seems and works to uncover the hidden forces that shape both the phenomena we encounter and the observer's frames of reference.

Poststructuralist feminism—a social-theoretical position that questions the universalizing tendencies of structural approaches to scholarship—e.g., Piaget's universal stages of child development or Maslow's hierarchy of needs. Thus, poststructuralism emphasizes the historical and cultural contextual contingencies of all human experience—child development for boys and girls in isolated tribal groups in Botswana may be different than with Swiss boys from the middle and upper-middle classes. In a poststructural context, language becomes extremely important as it culturally, socially and politically inscribes particular situations. As it uncovers these dynamics, poststructuralism fosters resistance to the power they exert in the regulation and discipline of individuals. In a feminist context, poststructuralist feminism has emphasized the diversity of women's experiences as opposed to their unity and sameness. In line with larger poststructuralist theory, women in this theoretical construct do not constitute a single group but are differentiated by race, class, sexuality, historical context and ethnicity.

Structural coupling—involves recurring interactions that lead to structural interactions between two or more systems. The concept is very important in enactivism and complexity theory in the effort to explain the ways that complex systems develop.

CHAPTER FOUR

Representing the World

Analyzing the Construction Zone

Point 9: Critical constructivists assert that understanding the positioning of the researcher in the social web of reality is essential to the production of rigorous and textured knowledge. As long as researchers and consumers of knowledge do not understand where they themselves and other researchers stand in this social web, scholars will have a thin and distorted conception of the research process and the data it produces.

One of the most compelling elements of critical constructivism involves the development of a dynamic appreciation of the way power works at both macro (deep structural) and micro (particularistic) levels to shape our understandings of the role and our role in it. Such theoretical work might begin its analysis of macro-power with Gramscian notions of hegemony and its analysis of micro-power with the Foucauldian notion of discursive construction with its intrapersonal and interpersonal dimensions. The theoretical innovation critical constructivism seeks involves the identification of "contact points" where these macro and micro manifestations of power connect. The search for these contact points takes place on the individual terrain of consciousness, necessitating, in a sense, a **phenomenology** of power—in a Foucauldian sense an archaeology of consciousness.

Phenomenology
the study of phenomena in the world as they are constructed by our consciousness. As it analyzes such phenomena, it asks what makes something what it is. In this way phenomenologists "get at" the meaning of lived experience, the meaning of experience as we live it. In this effort phenomenology attempts to study what it means to be human.

These contact points can always be found in archaeological excavations of artifacts of researcher positionality—where she stands or is placed in the social web of reality. Such explorations of researcher consciousness are central to critical constructivism's effort to expose the worldview she or he takes for granted. Here critical constructivist researchers begin to appreciate the subtle ways power shapes their research, their methods of constructing data and interpretations of it, and their narrative voice. With this insight they begin to reconstruct their perception of the world in a manner that prepares them not only to deconstruct what has always appeared natural but also to rethink the ways in which they present their social and cultural reformulations to their readers (Lincoln and Guba, 1985; Noblit, 1985, 1999; Slaughter, 1989; Denzin and Lincoln, 2000).

Critical constructivism openly attempts to subvert the researcher's perception of her stable location in the web of reality. Researchers with objectivist stable self-perceptions often control their interpretations of the world so as to protect their coherence and consistency. The narratives that ensue aspire to a naïve realist mimetic (imitational) representation of the already existing world. Whatever the intention, the cosmos represented is one of the researchers' own construction, typically a bounded reality that derives its closure from the solution to the puzzle. The questioning of researcher positionality undermines such facile resolutions, such glib constructions. Such questions do not encourage a view that denies researcher agency or self-direction. Indeed, researchers act intentionally, but the perceptions and appreciations that inform their actions are inscribed by the social and the political. From the critical constructivist's perspective, the challenge involves understanding the ways researchers' potential fields of action are constructed and how such constructions are addressed in the formulation of the research act (Donald, 1993).

The power field that helps construct the researcher does not contribute to the construction of a unified and stable positionality. No hermeneutic closure awaits the last word of the researcher's narrative; no final reading/construction of the *Lebenswelt* (life-world) brings the story to a tidy ending. Like a 1950s sci-fi movie about ants transformed into gargantuan killers by atomic radiation, "the end" becomes "the end?"—what will be the next species to mutate as a response to the by-products of modernist science? The sci-fi screenwriters didn't think about epistemological science fiction, where scientific knowledge production shaped by its complicity with power distorts our views of the world and self to the point we harm our most vulnerable citizens, destroy the environment and undermine the quality of life around the world. All of this we accept under the justification of promoting "American democracy and values."

Feminist theory's notion of voice when filtered by poststructuralist insight—the understanding that women are not the same everywhere and that gender must always be viewed in a racial, class, national, sexual and religious context—helps us negotiate the discomfort produced by critical constructivism's encounter with open-ended and complex positionality. Such a conception of voice depicts it not as independent and preexistent but forged out of the individual's discursive and semiotic interplay with the power of patriarchy, racism, class bias and other social forces. Thus, an individual does not discover a voice that was there all the time but constructs one in negotiation with her environment. In the context of inquiry, critical constructivism intervenes in the construction process by pointing out the omnipresence of power. Thus, an informed voice is fashioned that is empowered to speak/write in the cause of social justice, egalitarian social change and rigorous scholarship.

The Construction Process: Discourse, Language and Power

Too rarely do we analyze the deep social assumptions and power relations embedded in everyday language. School in general and the study of research in particular fails to question the ways unexamined language shapes education, the research about it and the narrative format that transmits it to the reader. Critical constructivists aware of these dynamics advocate not only linguistic analysis of research traditions but autobiographical studies of the student researcher. The emphasis of such studies center around self-reflection and the construction of (un)consciousness. The narratives emerging from such a self-conscious researcher would be far more attuned to the nuance of representation and the ideological and epistemological dimensions of narrative format. Both language and literary forms are inscribed by the language of the power bloc. Creations of particular narrative forms and certain fiction formulas mobilize meanings that often sustain domination. Any critical constructivist reading of a text—fiction or nonfiction—examines language, narrative and representation in the light of these power plays (Thompson, 1987; Suvin, 1988; Probyn, 1993; Fiske, 1993; Denzin and Lincoln, 2000).

Discourse analysis
The study of discourses where a discourse is defined as a constellation of hidden historical rules that govern what can be and cannot be said and who can speak and who must listen. Discursive practices are present in technical processes, institutions and modes of behavior and in their forms of transmission and representation. Discourses shape how we operate in the world as human agents, construct our consciousness, and what we consider true.

Traditional ethnographies, for example, have been comfortable with the supposition that language neutrally conveys a description of reality. Critical constructivist researchers understand that linguistic descriptions are not as much *about* society as they are *constitutive* of the social cosmos—that is, they create reality. Borrowing from **discourse analysis**, critical constructivists understand language as the substance of social action, not simply the reflection of it. Objectivist ethnography assumed that as a neutral medium, language could be refined to the point that a "proper" ethnographic vocabulary could be developed. From this professional lexicon, objective representations of the social world could be generated that would legitimate ethnography as a "hard" scientific enterprise. Once such a project is abandoned and the constituent aspects of language are understood, critical researchers can embark on a quest for new literary strategies that break down the addiction to authorial certainty. In such a context readers are invited into a dialogue between researcher and researched where former hierarchies and formal methodological artifices of positivist science are relegated to the junk pile of epistemological history (Derrida, 1976; Foucault, 1980; Agger, 1992; Sherrard, 1991; Gubrium and Holstein, 2000; Fontana, 1994; Kincheloe, 2003).

All language is multiaccentual, meaning that it can both be spoken and heard, written and read in ways that reflect different meanings and different relationships to social groups and power formations. When language is used in a dominant power-driven imperializing manner—meaning as a form of social regulation—this multiaccentual dimension is repressed. Power wielders attempt to establish one correct meaning among listeners or readers in an effort to implant a particular ideological message into their consciousness. Such a linguistic act is an example of what is labeled discursive closure—a language game that represses alternate ways of seeing as it establishes a textual orthodoxy. For example, "When the Lord spoke to the Apostle Paul in this vision, it meant that God wanted men to rule over women in the home, family and the marketplace." The interpreter here uses the discourse of divine authority to tell his listeners what the Bible as a text really meant. No further discussion is necessary.

In this way discourses define what is normal and deviant, what is the *proper* way of constructing reality and what is not. Indeed, this process of definition, inclusion, and exclusion connects discourse to modes of social ordering and of regulation of knowledge production. For example, mainstream research discourses avoid representations of the concept of oppression when examining questions of justice or injustice. Often terms such as discrimination or prejudice are used to represent race, class and gender injustice—the concept of oppression, being a much more inclusive and damning concept, is inappropriate in a discourse complicit with the dominant power bloc (Young, 1992; Fiske, 1993; Brown, 1994; Kincheloe and Steinberg, 1997). Thus, discursive closure is effected; the status quo is protected. In such contexts of discursive closure, there is no need to analyze researcher position. It doesn't matter who you are; there are correct constructions and incorrect ones.

Point 10: In the critical constructivist process of reconstructing the self, humans are ethically required to search in as many locations as possible for unique ideas, alternative discourses, new ways of thinking and being intelligent, and producing knowledge—the explosive power of difference.

Critical constructivists see difference as a kinetic form of social, political, epistemological, and pedagogical energy. Difference in the critical constructivist context is a tool to change the world, not only a concept connected to issues of toleration and diversity. Engaging difference in its lived expression so that social inquiry is connected to action in the world, critical constructivists engage in knowledge work grounded upon a transformative politics of difference. In this context researchers study the ways difference is constructed by historical and social processes, in particular the ways power works to shape the meaning and lived expression of difference. In this context critical researchers work to set up what Ray Horn (2000) calls postformal conversations, where differences are acknowledged and used to address individual needs and systemic inequities. All cultural groups differ in profound ways. Knowing this, critical constructivists who engage in the postformal conversation assume a radical humility that leads to a spirit of equality. Such a disposition allows such transformative scholars the opportunity to begin the daunting task of developing genuine and egalitarian interactions among the various cultures of the planet (Richardson and Woolfolk, 1994; Giroux, 1997a; Allen, 2000). Based on this foundation the research in which they engage harbors a vision of what could be in the realms of race, class, gender, sexuality and culture.

Thus, critical constructivists make organic connections with social, cultural and historical traditions in a manner informed by understanding the power relations that shape them. In addition, they are aware of where they stand in relation to these important power relations—as in our discussion of positionality. With this insight they are better prepared to use the knowledges they produce to initiate critical action. Informed by local knowledges from multiple social and cultural locations, critical constructivists avoid the grand narratives of Western discourses that are monological in their dismissal of histories and the cultural concerns of non-Western peoples. In this context they are able to make use of multiple generative narratives emerging from diverse locales that are dedicated to the production of new ways of making meaning and being/becoming human. Difference in this context is negotiated in the womb of solidarity. These multiple generative narratives are central to the bricolage. Such narratives—as we have illustrated throughout *Critical Constructivism*—might include poststructuralist feminism, **postcolonial** discourses, various social theoretical analyses of macro-social structures vis-à-vis interactionist understandings of micro-dimensions of everyday life, critical hermeneutical ways of interpreting, Santiago enactivist cognitive theories, etc.

Postcolonialism in the most technical sense the term refers to the period after colonial rule, but there are many dimensions of postcolonialism that transcend this meaning. In a critical constructivist context one of those dimensions involves examining and working through the effects of colonialism in the political, social, cultural, economic and educational spheres of both colonizer and colonized states and peoples.

Researchers who employ this transformative politics of difference, however, understand the difficulty of producing critical knowledges. In a globalized era marred by historical and contemporary power asymmetries, researchers interested in using their knowledges for social change face daunting obstacles. Difference in such contexts too often leads directly to tension and violence. In the post-9/11 landscape dominated by U.S. military power, tension and violence escalate. From the international level to the national and local domains, difference in the twenty-first century is often not viewed as an opportunity for insight and social and personal transformation. Indeed, diversity without conversation, community or a web of relationships can lead to hatred and misunderstanding. If a sense of the interdependence of all peoples has not been established, difference can lead to conflict and murder. In a situation where particular power groups have dominated specific peoples for centuries—as in European and U.S. colonialism and neo-colonialism—the possibility for conflict increases many-fold. In this context difference for the colonized signifies the taking of their political, social, epistemological, educational and economic power and the imposition of an alien culture.

European knowledges in these colonial and neo-colonial contexts are often presented to the colonial other as the one correct point of view, as discursive closures. The knowledges of the colonized are demonized and viewed as inherently inferior. Difference is viewed as a marker of deficiency. Indeed, in an epistemological context more voices are not viewed as a benefit but as a cacophony of confusion undermining the scientific effort to get the correct answer. As such rationalism relegates the local knowledge of those low in status to the margins, it guarantees that official knowledge remains monological and unblemished by difference. In such a monological context Europeans could produce universal knowledge about the "true nature" of the world and its people. Using such knowledge to build theories delineating proper human behavior and development, Europeans gained the power to tell others what to do, how to organize their lives. Employing a transformative politics of difference, critical constructivists seek to throw a monkey wrench into such mechanistic operations (Allen, 2000; Degenaar, 1995; Thayer-Bacon, 2000; Thomas, 1998).

Such researchers make sure that Western rationalism is removed from its sacred sanctuary as the only legitimate mode of knowledge production. They take rationalism into the epistemological bazaar, where it assumes its place as simply another way of making meaning and producing knowledge about the world. Here it coexists with traditions coming from different places and times. It encounters modes of perceiving that utilize both rational and emotional dynamics and make use of context and interrelationship in unique ways. Critical constructivists like to hang out in the epistemological bazaar listening to and picking up on articulations of subjugated knowledges. In the bazaar of knowledge they can engage in unimagined conversations that move them to new levels of insight derived from juxtaposing diverse forms of meaning-making.

In addition to different cultural knowledges and modes of meaning-making, critical constructivists study the history of European academic disciplines and the insights to be gained from traditions of dissent within such disciplines. Here they study the relationship of canonical and counter-canonical ways of seeing. In this interactive setting they are less interested in asking about the truth of other traditions and more concerned with inquiring about the origins of such perspectives and their implications for the larger act of knowledge production. Such questions ignite a powerful intellectual experience that pushes research, knowledge production and pedagogy to new horizons (Pickering, 1999; Thayer-Bacon, 2000; Degenaar, 1995; Allen, 2000).

Back to Postformalism: Cognition, Knowledge Production and Difference.

As discussed in Chapter 3, postformalism provides an important foundation for any notion of a critical constructivist cognition informed by difference. The way we conceptualize cognition exerts a profound impact on both the goals of our research and the everyday activities of researchers. Do we think of the mind as a computer that files representations of the world to be accessed when needed? Or do we view the mind in a more complex manner as an entity that constructs knowledge as it interacts with the world and other knowledge producers? As a complex model for a form of thinking that takes seriously the critique of Cartesian rationalism and the critical constructivist effort to deploy the power of difference, postformalism can change the direction of epistemological work. In research shaped by scholars who understand postformalism and the type of analysis that can emerge from it, self-reflection leads inquirers to become detectives of both intelligence and forms of knowledge work in diverse contexts, both academic and outside of academia.

The alternative cognitive practices that emerge in these diverse contexts are often grounded in cooperative interaction between and among diverse peoples. In this cooperative domain individuals are privy to the various forms of interrelatedness. Attending to the characteristics of such connections, individuals come to see order instead of chaos. The concept of interconnection moves postformalists to bring Humberto Maturana and Francisco Varela's cognitive theory of enactivism into the bricolage. In such interconnections and the patterns and processes enfolded within them, we begin to discern one of the most amazing phenomena uncovered in recent times. Francisco Varela (1999) writes that as unlikely as it may seem

> Lots of simple agents having simple properties may be brought together, even in a haphazard way, to give rise to what appears to be a purposeful and integrated whole, without the need for central supervision (p. 52).

In this simple statement we begin to uncover a whole new dimension of not only cognitive activity but also of the character of "the self." In this domain we blaze new trails into the epistemological and ontological domains. In the epistemological domain we begin to realize that knowledge is stripped of its meaning when it stands alone. This holds profound implications in research because European science has studied the world in a way that isolates the object of study, abstracts it from the contexts and interrelationships that give it meaning. Thus, to be a researcher in a manner that takes Varela's enactivist notion into account, we have to study the world "in context." Critical constructivists understand that they have to search for the interrelationships and contexts that give knowledge meaning while avoiding reliance upon decontextualized study. The notion of difference directly references the relationship of different entities. Thus, the critical constructivist concern with difference gains its cognitive and epistemological power in these relationships.

Of course, this cognitive and epistemological power of difference is being subverted in the beginning of the twenty-first century by the emergence of an American Empire that privileges one way of seeing and one vision of both history and the future. Because a central dimension of the Empire involves the monological production and control of information, possibilities for encountering difference continue to decline. In this context we begin to realize that cognition cannot be separated from the political and the epistemological. Such recognitions are central to the application of critical constructivism in social, political, psychological and educational research. Drawing upon the contextual and perspectival dimensions of knowledge production, such researchers understand that we are all dependent on our relationships with others—the power of difference—to facilitate our effort to transcend the blinders of our own limited perspectives. Making use of difference becomes a prerequisite for rigorous research and knowledge work.

Indeed, critical constructivists refuse to be confined to one cultural way of seeing and making meaning. In contemporary society they organize communities of conceptual difference operating at a macro-level much like the mind operates in the interaction of its various parts. Thus, difference is expanded into concepts such as the web of life and the web of social, cultural and political reality into which all humans fit. Critical scholars, thus, work to make use of the relationships one encounters in these webs—relationships that were torn apart by the Cartesian fragmentation of the world and its effort to tame difference. Taking their cue from enactivists, critical constructivists view cognition as a reflection of life processes in general. Such life processes used physical diversity to form interrelationships that led to more complex biological processes. An understanding of human cognition based on relationship operates in a similar way, establishing interactions with different entities to produce more complex understandings of self and world.

One's cognitive development as a critical constructivist researcher, therefore, would require that one seek out difference in multiple historical, cultural, psychological, philosophical, political, social, economic and educational contexts. One of the most important tasks involves bringing together diverse individuals and traditions for the purpose of producing a synergistic postformal conversation between them (Horn, 2000). Again drawing upon the work of Maturana and Varela (1987), bricoleurs study the way the complexity of an ecosystem's web of relationships is connected to its biodiversity. In this context biologists have come to recognize that a diverse ecological community is more resistant to destruction than a more homogenous ecological community—a central concept in critical constructivism's use of difference.

In human communities, especially in the domains of cognition and epistemology, we may find similar dynamics at work. In these domains difference involves analyzing and understanding a plethora of relationships between numerous concepts. It involves engaging, for example, diverse approaches to the same problem. In this way cognitive activity and knowledge production are strengthened, as new insights and ways of pursuing knowledge emerge in the interaction of different approaches (Williams, 1999; Murphie, 1998; O'Sullivan, 1999; Capra, 1996).

Whenever physical systems are used to provide insight into social systems, caution is necessary. Nevertheless, the use of Maturana and Varela's biological insights may be helpful in understanding the ways difference operates in social, cognitive and epistemological systems. I am aware that such interpretations must be offered with the knowledge that they are constructions developed at a particular historical moment in a particular historical setting. In this context it is important to study the role of difference in self-organizing systems. According to Maturana and Varela, self-organization is not possible without difference. In autopoietic systems, an entity evolves by reaching out into novelty and constructing synergistic interactions, not by chance mutations and natural selection. Life forms unfold in relation to their exposure to multiple levels of diversity in a manner that can be described as a creative cognitive process. Drawing upon these concepts, critical constructivist researchers reach out for novelty in the social, cultural, political, economic, philosophical and economic domains.

Even the notion of autopoietic biology itself was developed by connecting biology to non-Western philosophical traditions. Connecting with difference is central in all of these situations. In enactivist biology humans are seen as engaging in a continuous and egalitarian dialogue with the physical world rather than in a unidirectional monologue. Drawing on the Taoist notion that the physical world emerges from the cooperation of all living and non-living things in their diversity, Maturana and Varela theorized life processes and cognitive processes as similar in form and function. Knowing what we know about the role of difference in shaping these processes, only a regressive ethnocentrism prevents Western researchers from making use of the unique insights of Islam, Hinduism, Buddhism, African traditions and other indigenous modes of meaning-making. As critical constructivists are coming to realize, these traditions provide tremendous insights into the effort to make sense of and change the contemporary world. When such ways of seeing are brought together with a rigorous power, profound epistemological and ontological synergies emerge that further empower the work of the critical constructivist scholars and educators (Varela, 1999; Capra, 1996; Pickering, 1999; O'Sullivan, 1999).

Approaching Self-Awareness via the Power of Difference

When critical constructivists encounter difference in the nature of the other they enter into symbiotic relationships where the identity of the researcher is changed. The researchers are no longer merely obtaining information but are entering a space of transformation where previously excluded perspectives operate to change consciousness of both self and the world. Thus, critical constructivist research changes not only what one knows but who one actually is. Thus, the epistemological and ontological domains enter into a new relationship that produces dramatic changes. Lev Vygotsky was on the right track as he documented the importance of the context in which learning takes place—the zone of proximal development (ZPD). Difference in the sense we are using it here expands the notion of the ZPD into the domain of research, drawing upon the power of our interactions in helping shape the ways we make meaning. In the new synergized position, critical researchers construct new realities where they take on new and expanded roles.

Aware of the power of difference, such researchers develop a new consciousness of the self: 1) the manner in which it has been constructed; 2) its limitations; and 3) a sense of immanence concerning what it can become. Self-awareness is a metacognitive skill that has historically been more valued in Eastern traditions such as Buddhism, Taoism and Yoga than in the West. Time and again we see the value of pluralism manifest itself in this discussion of difference and critical constructivism. A pluralistic epistemology helps us understand the way we are situated in the web of reality and how this situatedness constructs what we see as researchers. Such an awareness reveals the limited nature of our observations of the world. Instead of researchers making final pronouncements on the way things are, they begin to see themselves in a larger interdisciplinary and intercultural conversation. In this context they begin to focus their attention on better modes of listening and respecting diverse viewpoints. Such higher-order listening moves them to new levels of self-consciousness (Williams, 1999; Newland, 1997; Lepani, 1998; Thayer-Bacon, 2000).

Of course, difference does not work as an invisible hand that magically shapes new insights into self and world. Humans must exercise their hermeneutic abilities to forge these connections and interpret their meanings. In this context critical constructivists confront difference and then decide where they stand in relation to it. They must discern what to make of what it has presented them. With this in mind they work hard to develop relationships with those different from themselves who operate to create new meanings in the interactions of identity and difference. In this interaction they grow smarter as they reject modernist Cartesian notions that cultural conflicts can be solved only by developing monological universal principles of epistemology and universal steps to the process of research. Too often, of course, such "universal" principles simply reflect colonial Western ways of viewing the world hiding in the disguise of universalism. Rigorous examinations of the construction of self and society are closed off in such faux-universalism. Indeed, it undermines the development of a critical self-consciousness.

In the face of a wide variety of different knowledges and ways of seeing the world, the cosmos human beings think they know collapses. In a counter-colonial move, critical constructivists raise questions about any knowledges and ways of knowing that claim universal status. In this context bricoleurs make use of this suspicion of universalism in combination with global knowledges to understand how they have been positioned in the world. Almost all of us from Western backgrounds or non-Western colonized backgrounds have been implicated in some way in the web of universalism. The inevitable conflicts that arise from this implication do not have to be resolved immediately. At the base of these conflicts rests the future of global culture as well as the future of rigorous and just research and pedagogy. Appreciating that these are generative issues that engage us in a productive process of analyzing self and world is in itself a powerful recognition. The value of both this recognition and the process of working through the complicated conceptual problems are treasured by critical constructivists. Indeed, they avoid any notion of finality in the resolution of such dilemmas (Richardson and Woolfolk, 1994; Degenaar, 1995; Howley, Pendarvis and Howley, 1993; O'Sullivan, 1999; Fenwick, 2000). In the context the future of knowledge production and human intercultural relationships can be changed.

The Subversive Nature of Difference: Respecting the Margins

Critical constructivism accepts the subversive notion that human experience is marked by uncertainties and that order is not always easily established. "Order in the court" has little authority when the monological judge is resting in *his* quarters. Indeed, the rationalistic and reductionistic quest for order refuses in its arrogance to listen to the cacophony of lived experience, the coexistence of diverse meanings and interpretations, and the diverse voices in the bazaar. The concept of understanding in the complex world viewed by critical constructivists is unpredictable. Much to the consternation of many, there exists no final transhistorical, non-ideological meaning that researchers strive to achieve. As critical constructivist researchers construct rather than discover meaning in enacted reality, they explore alternate meanings offered by others in similar circumstances. If this weren't enough, they work to account for historical and social contingencies that always operate to undermine the universal pronouncement of the meaning of a particular phenomenon. When researchers fail to discern the unique ways that historical and social context make for special circumstances, they often provide a reductionistic form of knowledge that impoverishes our understanding of everything connected to it—the process of research included (Burbules and Beck, 1999; Marijuan, 1994; Cary, 2004).

The monological quest for order so desired by many social, political, psychological and educational researchers is grounded on the Cartesian belief that all phenomena should be broken down into their constituent parts to facilitate inquiry. The analysis of the world in this context becomes fragmented and disconnected. Everything is studied separately for the purposes of rigor. The goal of integrating knowledges from diverse domains and understanding the interconnections shaping, for example, the biological and the cognitive, is irrelevant in the objectivist paradigm of order and fragmentation. The meaning that comes from interrelationship is lost, and questions concerning the purpose of research and its insight into the human condition are put aside in an orgy of correlation and triangulated description. Information is sterilized, and insight into what may be worth exploring is abandoned (Simpson and Jackson, 2001). Ways of making use of particular knowledge are viewed as irrelevant, and creative engagement with conceptual insights is characterized as frivolous. Empirical knowledge in the quest for order is an end in itself. Once it has been validated it needs no further investigation or interpretation. While empirical research is obviously necessary, its process of production constitutes only one step of a larger and more rigorous process of inquiry. Critical constructivism subverts the finality of the empirical act.

Empirical research, all research for that matter, is inscribed at every level by human beings. The assumptions and purposes of the researcher always find their way into a research act, and they always make a difference in what knowledge is produced. Even in the most prescribed forms of empirical quantitative inquiry, the researcher's preferences and assumptions shape the outcome of the research. Do I choose factor analysis or regression analysis to study the relationship of a student's SAT score to college success? The path I choose profoundly affects what I find. What about the skills and knowledges included on the SAT? Are they simply neutral phenomena free from inscriptions of culture and power? How I answer such a question shapes how my research proceeds.

Such inscriptions and the complexity they produce remind critical constructivists of the multiple processes in play when knowledge is produced and validation is considered. They understand that the research process is subjective, and instead of repressing this subjectivity, they attempt to understand its role in shaping inquiry. All of these elements come together to help them think about their principles of selection of one or another research perspective. Such decisions can be made more thoughtfully when a researcher understands the preferences and assumptions inscribed on all modes of inquiry and all individuals who engage in research. Thus, an important aspect of the work of the critical constructivist knowledge producer involves coming to understand the social construction of self, the influence of selfhood on perception, and the influence of perception on the nature of inquiry (Richardson and Woolfolk, 1994; Pickering, 1999; Allen, 2000).

Such concerns set up the critical constructivist move to the social margins. Such insight helps researchers reshape and sophisticate social theory, research methods and interpretive strategies as they discern new topics to be researched. This confrontation with difference enables researchers to produce new forms of knowledge that inform policy decisions and political action in general. In gaining this insight from the margins, critical constructivist researchers display once again the blurred boundary between the hermeneutical search for understanding and the critical concern with social change for social justice. Understanding and the pursuit of social change and social justice are not only not in conflict, they are synergistic (McLaren, Hammer, Reilly and Sholle, 1995; DeVault, 1996; Lutz, Jones and Kendall, 1997; Soto, 2000; Steinberg, 2001).

To contribute to social transformation, critical constructivists seek to better understand both the forces of domination that affect the lives of individuals from race, class, gender, sexual, ethnic and religious backgrounds outside of dominant culture(s) and the worldviews of such diverse peoples. In this context bricoleurs attempt to remove knowledge construction and its benefits from the control of elite groups. Such control consistently operates to reinforce elite privilege while pushing marginalized groups farther away from the center of dominant power. Rejecting this normalized state of affairs, they commit their knowledge work to helping address the ideological and informational needs of marginalized groups and individuals. As detectives of subjugated insight, bricoleurs eagerly learn from labor struggles, women's marginalization, the "double consciousness" of the racially oppressed and insurrections against colonialism (Young and Yarbrough, 1993; Kincheloe and Steinberg, 1993; Kincheloe, Steinberg and Hinchey, 1999).

Thus, critical constructivism is dedicated to a form of rigor that is conversant with numerous modes of meaning-making and knowledge production—modes that originate in diverse social locations. These alternative modes of reasoning and researching always consider the relationships, the resonances and the disjunctions between formal and rationalistic modes of Western epistemology and ontology and different cultural, philosophical, paradigmatic, and subjugated expressions. In these latter expressions critical constructivists often uncover ways of accessing a concept without resorting to a conventional validated set of pre-specified procedures that provide the distance of objectivity. This notion of distance fails to take into account the rigor of the production of hermeneutical understanding of the way meaning is pre-inscribed in the act of being in the world, the research process and objects of research. This absence of hermeneutical awareness undermines the researcher's quest for a thick description and contributes to the production of reduced understandings of the complexity of social life (Selfe and Selfe, 1994; Paulson, 1995).

The multiple perspectives delivered by the concept of difference provide researchers with many benefits as they weave their way through different research orientations and theoretical dimensions. Confrontation with difference helps us to see anew, to move toward the light of epiphany. A basic dimension of criticality involves a comfort with the existence of alternative ways of analyzing and producing knowledge. This is why it's so important for a historian, for example, to develop an understanding of phenomenology and hermeneutics. It is why it is so important for a social researcher from New York City to understand forms of indigenous African knowledge production. The incongruities between such cultural modes of inquiry are quite valuable, for within the tensions of difference rest insights into multiple dimensions of the research act—insights that move us to new levels of understanding of the subjects, purposes, and nature of inquiry (Semali and Kincheloe, 1999; Burbules and Beck, 1999).

Difference pushes us into the hermeneutic circle as we are induced to deal with parts in their diversity in relation to the whole. Difference may involve culture, class, language, discipline, epistemology, cosmology, ad infinitum. Critical constructivists use one dimension of these multiple diversities to explore others, to generate questions previously unimagined. As we examine these multiple perspectives, we attend to which ones are validated and which ones have been dismissed. Studying such differences we begin to understand how dominant power operates to exclude and certify particular forms of knowledge production and why. This focus on power and difference always leads us to an awarecness of the multiple dimensions of the social. Paulo Freire (1970) referred to this as the need for perceiving social structures and social systems that undermine equal access to resources and power. As critical constructivists answer such questions, we gain new appreciations of the way power tacitly shapes what we know and how we come to know it.

One of the best examples of the use of the power of difference in innovative contemporary scholarship involves Maturana and Varela's work in the development of enactivist cognitive theory. As it combines the disciplinary perspectives of biology, psychology, theology, philosophy and socio-cultural insights, enactivism works to address the fragmentation of modernist psychology. Drawing upon the Western philosophical scholarship of Merleau-Ponty and Heidegger and the Buddhist philosophy of **Nagarjuna**, enactivism integrates ways of knowing that are profoundly separated temporally and spatially to create

Nagarjuna
one of the most important philosophers in the Buddhist tradition. Living in the second and third centuries, Nagarjuna founded the Mahayanal school of Buddhism. In this school he taught a philosophy that rejected all opposites and sought what came to be known as the Middle Way.

a new synthesis. In the case of enactivism, cognitive studies is viewed from the perspectives of other traditions to create new approaches to theorizing and researching the topic as well as to gain a new understanding of the complexity and multi-dimensionality of the cognitive act (Carter, 2004; Pickering, 1999; Thayer-Bacon, 2000).

Tara Fenwick (2000) takes this enactivist insight to a higher level of interdisciplinarity as she integrates it with constructivist epistemological, critical theoretical and psychological discourses. I have attempted a similar strategy in my work in critical thinking (Kincheloe, 2003). Such interdisciplinary work, Fenwick contends, can not only provide new insights but can confront each perspective with new questions. Such questions can lead to dramatic advances at the frontiers where the diverse perspectives intersect.

Another example of the use of bricolage involves James Lovelock and Lynn Margulis's (1974) Gaia theory. Lovelock and Margulis study life in a systemic manner, drawing upon geology, microbiology, atmospheric chemistry, philosophy, sociology and other disciplines of inquiry that operate typically in isolation. Gaia theory questions the dominant Cartesian viewpoint that the aforementioned disciplines are discrete and separate and that geological dynamics alone created the context for the evolution of life on our planet. Valuing the input of diverse disciplines, Lovelock and Margulis challenged geology's longstanding claim that plants and animals were secondary entities who serendipitously found geological conditions congenial to their development and evolution. Instead, Lovelock and Margulis's research indicated that life produces the conditions that enable its own existence. In this context the researchers contended that the surface of the planet, long viewed as the environment in which life developed, is actually a dimension of life. Instead of life merely adapting to an inert physical environment, living things in fact construct the environment with which they interact. Life and its environment feed back on one another, modifying each other in the complexity of the living process. Without the tensions produced by a bricolage of perspectives, such a new view of the nature of life could not have been conceived (Capra, 1996).

One final example of the employment of the power of difference and one that directly influences our articulation of its meaning here is, of course, in cultural studies. Advocates of cultural studies believe that the study of culture is fragmented among a variety of disciplines—sociology, anthropology, history, literary studies, communications, etc.—to the point that communication among scholars is undermined. This is a fragmentary dynamic that has always adversely affected the work of cultural scholars. Cultural studies as a trans-discipline attempts to overcome this fragmentation by highlighting culture as a living process that shapes the ways we live, view ourselves, and understand the world around us. Scholars of cultural studies argue that by adopting cultural studies' overtly multidisciplinary approach, researchers can study larger social issues, such as race, class, gender, sexuality, ethnicity, immigration and pedagogy from unique perspectives and theoretical positions. As students of cultural studies question the dominant ways of seeing that evolve around the normal science of disciplinary thinking, they free themselves from the self-validating redundancies that limit insight and chain them to familiar explanations (Kincheloe, 2001).

The subversive element of critical constructivism takes these examples and uses them in the larger struggle for social justice and the democratization of everyday life. There is no reason that scholars should be the only individuals with access to the power of difference. Practitioners such as teachers, social workers, journalists, nurses, business people and other individuals should most definitely make use of this power. To make critical constructivist scholarship the exclusive province of the elite is to perpetuate the same forms of power and privilege that have marred and scarred everyday life in Western societies for centuries. Humans are meaning-making life forms and need to be involved in experiences that help us sophisticate our ability to do so. Critical constructivist difference provides a beginning framework for helping all people in all walks of life construct systems of meaning-making. Such systems grant us ways of producing knowledge that help us make sense of the species' past as well as our own personal past. Such knowledge empowers us to construct a more equitable, exciting, just and intelligent future.

Facing the diversity of knowledges of multiple pasts and possible futures, critical constructivists transcend reductionistic modes of fragmented knowledge production that deny the socially constructed nature of all research. The ways we conduct research are not given, immutable processes that contain no creative dimension. Critical constructivists take seriously our creative responsibility to break the lenses of present ways of viewing the world. Such lenses need to be broken not because of some Oedipal impulse to kill the father, but because such frames have caused such heartbreak and suffering on the part of those who fall outside the favored race, class, gender, sexual, religious and ability-related demographic. The blurred genres of critical constructivism highlight the mode of difference that creates new respect for the subjugated and the knowledges they produce. One dimension of the respect for difference promoted here involves forming new relationships—often learning relationships—with these previously dismissed and degraded forms of information and their producers. The new perspectives we gain from our deployment of difference demand new criteria for assessing the value of knowledge and knowledge production. Such criteria reflect a meta-awareness of the notion of value itself—a concept that demands reconceptualization in the new world of complexity encountered in the process of constructing and enacting the power of difference (Geeland and Taylor, 2000; Bruner, 1996).

Indeed, what we are concerned with here is nothing less than the quality of the knowledge we produce about the world. In this context we address both the reductionism of uninformed research methods and the quest for new ways of seeing. In the intersection of these concerns we uncover new insights into research and knowledge production, new forms of reason that are directly connected to specific contexts, practical forms of analysis that are informed by social theory and the concreteness of lived situations (Fischer, 1998). Understanding non-Western ways of knowing and the epistemologies of marginalized groups within Western societies, critical constructivists transcend regressive forms of reductionism. They see past reductionistic notions that researchers simply produce facts that correspond to external reality, information that is devoid of specific cultural values. With these understandings as valuable parts of their toolkits, critical constructivists as bricoleurs expand the envelope of social research, of what we can understand about the world. They are empowered to produce knowledge that can change the world.

Glossary

Discourse analysis—The study of discourses where a discourse is defined as a constellation of hidden historical rules that govern what can be and cannot be said and who can speak and who must listen. Discursive practices are present in technical processes, institutions and modes of behavior and in their forms of transmission and representation. Discourses shape how we operate in the world as human agents, construct our consciousness, and what we consider true.

Nagarjuna—one of the most important philosophers in the Buddhist tradition. Living in the second and third centuries, Nagarjuna founded the Mahayanal school of Buddhism. In this school he taught a philosophy that rejected all opposites and sought what came to be known as the Middle Way.

Phenomenology—the study of phenomena in the world as they are constructed by our consciousness. As it analyzes such phenomena it asks what makes something what it is. In this way phenomenologists "get at" the meaning of lived experience, the meaning of experience as we live it. In this effort phenomenology attempts to study what it means to be human.

Postcolonialism—in the most technical sense the term refers to the period after colonial rule, but there are many dimensions of postcolonialism that transcend this meaning. In a critical constructivist context one of those dimensions involves examining and working through the effects of colonialism in the political, social, cultural, economic and educational spheres of both colonizer and colonized states and peoples.

CHAPTER FIVE

Blue Knowledge

Point 11: Critical constructivism works to expose elitist assumptions embedded in existing knowledge. Understanding that dominant power wielders have attempted to hegemonize individuals via the deployment of these knowledges in political economic, social, cultural, epistemological and pedagogical structures, many will be uncomfortable with the exposé process.

Critical constructivists know that academia can be an elite domain. Indeed, schools are often designed to intimidate and belittle students from diverse backgrounds. Many a day as a student I was ridiculed by teachers and professors attempting to discredit my efforts to make personal sense of lessons they were teaching. My inability to see the worlds of science, literature, history, or politics in the same way they presented them, often motivated my teachers to denigrate my intellectual ability. Friends of mine who also came from low-status backgrounds experienced similar treatment. I was the lucky one, however.

Despite teachers' protests to the contrary, I didn't think I was stupid.

The definitions of intelligence and performance employed are not generated by the marginalized. When liberals attempt, for example, to develop curricula or initiate research based on recognition of the existence of marginalized experiences, they miss the lessons provided by an understanding of subjugated knowledge, or as I will label it in this chapter "blue knowledge." A common liberal reform involves the inclusion of women or African Americans in a history curriculum that has traditionally emphasized the contributions of famous (especially military) men. In a traditional curricular framework this simply adds a few new facts to be committed to memory, it is a tokenism that perpetuates the power relations of the status quo (Kincheloe and Steinberg, 1997). Another such reform might involve making sure that respondents to a survey include a percentage of women and minorities (Connell, 1989).

The advantage of subjugated perspectives, the view from below, involves what has been termed the "double consciousness" of the oppressed (Steinberg, 2001; King and Mitchell, 1995; Brown and Davis, 2000). If they are to survive, subjugated groups develop an understanding of those who control them (e.g., slaves' insight into the manners, eccentricities and fears of their masters); at the same time they are cognizant of the everyday mechanisms of oppression and the way such technologies shape their consciousness, their lived realities. Because of their class, race and gender positions, many educational researchers are insulated from the benefits of the double consciousness of the subjugated and are estranged from a visceral appreciation of suffering (Zappulla, 1997). Contemporary social organization, thus, is viewed through a lens that portrays it as acceptable.

Why would such researchers challenge research methods, modes of interpretation which justify the prevailing system of education (Mayers, 2001a, 2001b; Jardine, 1998; Ellis, 1998; Malewski, 2001a)? What lived experience would create an ethical dissonance within the minds of such researchers that would make them uncomfortable with the status quo? The oppressed—while often manipulated by mechanisms of power to accept injustice and to deny their own oppression—often use their pain as a motivation to find out what is not right and to discover alternative ways of constructing social and educational reality (Mies, 1982; Jaggar, 1983). Women's ways of knowing—when understood in a race, class, sexual, religious and ethnic context wary of essentialism—as a subjugated form of knowledge have initiated a virtual revolution in our conception of what we know and how we come to know it. Serious consideration of such subjugated ways of knowing transforms forever our conceptions of the relation of the knower to the known and the conceptualization and execution of the research act. The research questions we ask as critical constructivist researchers often find their sources in these subjugated epistemologies.

Moving on to Critical Constructivism's Terrain of Uncertainty: The Postformal Perspective

Critical constructivist analysis has consistently laid bare the assumptions of Cartesian logic by illustrating the ways that the structure of traditional science constructs imaginary worlds. Like a novel, science is "written"; both the novel and science operate according to the arbitrary rules of a language game. Such understandings confront us with a dramatic socio-educational dilemma: how do we function in the midst of such uncertainty? Critical constructivism offers us aid in our dilemma—not salvation, just help. Using a critical theoretical system of meaning, tempering it with a dose of reflective self-analysis and epistemological humility, we take critical constructivism one more step. In this stride we conceptualize a democratic form of knowledge production which leads to a new way of seeing, a postformal way of perceiving the educational world (Kincheloe and Steinberg, 1993; Kincheloe, Steinberg and Hinchey, 1999; Horn, 2000).

What are the limits of human ways of knowing? Where might we go from here? Such questions have both research and pedagogical implications. Drawing upon our knowledge of critical constructivism, we cannot help but anticipate ways of knowing and levels of cognition which move beyond Cartesian convention and Piagetian formalism. Adults do not reach a final cognitive equilibrium beyond which no new levels of thought can emerge; there have to be modes of thinking which transcend the formal operational ability to formulate abstract conclusions, understand cause-effect relationships and employ the traditional scientific method to explain reality. We know too much to define formality as the zenith of human cognitive ability (Arlin, 1975).

Formalism implies an acceptance of a Cartesian-Newtonian mechanistic worldview trapped within a cause-effect system of reasoning. The formal operational thinker/researcher employs a science which breaks a social or educational system down into its basic parts in order to understand the way it works (Aronowitz, 1988,1996). Emphasizing certainty and prediction, formal operational thinking/researching organizes verified facts into a theory. The facts which do not fit into the theory are eliminated, and the theory developed is the one best suited to eliminate contradictions in knowledge. Thus, formal operational thought and its attendant mode of inquiry operate on the assumption that contradiction resolution is a central objective (Kramer, 1983). Schools and standardized test-makers, assuming that formal operational thought represents the highest level of human cognition, focus their efforts on its cultivation and measurement (though sometimes they fail to get too far beyond concrete forms of thinking) (Owen and Doerr, 1999). Students who have moved beyond formality are rarely rewarded and are sometimes even punished in educational contexts. Researchers who transcend formality have been severely criticized for their lack of rigor and their subjectivism.

Postformal thinkers/researchers are comfortable with the uncertain, tentative nature of knowledge emerging from critical constructivist research. They are tolerant of complexity and contradiction, and value the attempt to integrate ostensibly dissimilar phenomena into new, revealing syntheses. In other words, postformal thinkers/researchers escape the confines of Cartesian-Newtonian modernity and venture into a new cognitive and epistemological realm. Postformalism underpins a form of inquiry suitable for a hyperreal world: only a postformal thinker is cognitively and conceptually equipped to handle the uncertainty of our electronic hyperreality. Where the formal operational orientation functions on the basis of the Cartesian assumptions of linear causality and determinism, the postformal perspective assumes reciprocity and holism (the complex, nonlinear interconnection of events) (Van Hesteran, 1986; Kramer, 1983; Capra, 1996; O'Sullivan, 1999).

Thus, simple, privileged vantage points from which to view socio-educational phenomena are rejected by postformal thinkers, as they come to realize that there are many ways of approaching an event. Researchers will see multiple depictions of the phenomenon depending both on the context from which it emanates and the system of meaning they employ to help formulate their questions and research strategies—i.e., do they adopt a view from above or a view from below? Traditional Marxism argued in its own deterministic way that humans see only what their conceptual lenses allowed them to see and that they understand what the context for understanding permitted. In the spirit of hope, possibility and anti-determinism, critical constructivist researchers seek to liberate themselves from such determinism by taking control of our perceptual abilities, by transcending what the context permits.

In this way we emancipate ourselves from the constraints of the Cartesian dualism and the structural forces which limit our ability to see the world from outside our restricted vantage point. In its logocentrism, Cartesian modernity discounted the terrain of private inner reality (Pinar, 1994). What good was such a landscape in the process of industrialization, material progress, and the conquest of nature? As critical constructivists rediscover the sensuous, postformalism incorporates such notions into new ways of exploring and constructing the social, educational and even physical world (Gordon, Miller, and Rollock, 1990; Kramer, 1983; Slaughter, 1989; Kincheloe, Steinberg and Tippins, 1999).

Employing Discursive Analysis to Help Us Understand the New Uncertain Terrain

When it comes to the analysis of the construction of self or the nature of texts, critical constructivists are aware of the discursive practices in which self or text is embedded and the context in which self or text operates. Whether one is attempting to make sense of a novelist, an interviewee or a historical manuscript, discourse and context are central dimensions of the act of knowledge construction. Contrary to the pronouncements of some analysts, the contingent orientation to research created by such dimensions of knowledge production does not make one anti-empiricist or irrational. Instead such concerns make the critical constructivist more attentive to the various dynamics that construct what is called empirical knowledge. In this context such a researcher is less willing to make a final statement of truth or meaning based on the empirical investigations in which she has engaged. When empirical data are viewed from another perspective or questioned by one from a different or subjugated background, different interpretations can and often do emerge.

Discourse cannot be removed from power relations and the struggle to create particular meanings and legitimate specific voices. Dominant discourses shape the research process, emerging as technologies of power that regulate which knowledges are validated and which ones are relegated to the junk heap of history. As emphasized throughout this book, critical constructivists watch carefully as power operates to privilege the data coming from particular academic or political-economic locales. The insidious way this process operates is testimony to the axiom that power works best when it is not recognized as power. Power creeps in on little cats' feet to accomplish its regulation and discipline of various individuals and groups. Perceiving the world as we do through a shared culture and language, we tend to see phenomena in the ways those groups and individuals with the most power to construct our consciousnesses want us to. Of course, we resist such a process, but many times we are not even aware that it's operating. Indeed, it works best when everything seems normal and comfortable. Because it operates under the radar, pointing it out makes many individuals very uncomfortable. Consider the *Matrix* movies. Imagine how uncomfortable Keanu Reeves' character, Neo, is when he first learns of the existence of a constructed world, the matrix. While that matrix is fiction, the "matrix" of constructed reality critical constructivists lay out is not.

Power's construction of subjectivity and validation of particular forms of data take advantage of the comfort of the everyday. The production of meaning contrary to traditional rationalistic and dominant cultural notions is more tied to affective and emotional investments than previously realized. "I want to see myself as a 'man of science,' some researchers assert." As such a man I will produce hard, objective data that are becoming to such a respectable man." In such cases, we must ask what forces are at work in shaping the perspective this researcher takes toward social phenomena—rational deliberations or affective impulses? Critical constructivists maintain that such insights are important aspects of the research process and help us understand why particular interpretive and analytic perspectives are chosen both by themselves and by other researchers. With these ideas in mind critical constructivists ask "what is a fact?" Such a question takes on new layers of complexity and nuance when we think about the numerous contextual, discursive and power dynamics at work at every level of the processes that construct facts.

What exactly is it that is constructed as a product of this often bizarre and multidimensional process? Critical constructivists understand the multiple ways that a fact may be defined. They understand that it can viewed from many perspectives that grant it not only diverse meanings but different ontological statuses as well. From an ontological perspective, what is the nature of a fact? How does a fact operate in the world? And importantly, in this context, the critical constructivist scholar recognizes that given different contexts, discourses and power relations, what a researcher labels a fact could have been something fundamentally different. In this context we can project what alternative facts could have been produced given the reality of different contexts, discourses, and power relationships in the knowledge production process (Bruner, 1996; Giroux, 1997a; Hoban and Erickson, 1998; Capra, 1996). Such an intellectual ability, I believe, is a characteristic of rigorous scholarship.

The Social Theoretical Foundations of Critical Constructivism: Gaining Confidence on the Uncertain Terrain

Critical constructivists insist that in order to come to terms with the constructed nature of reality, it is essential for researchers, educators and their students to focus on the benefits of social theory. The questions asked and the concerns raised throughout this book have been driven by particular critical and other social theoretical dynamics. Contrary to positivist definitions of theory, these theoretical insights do not give us the true picture of the way the world operates. In a pedagogical context they do not tell teachers the correct way to teach. Instead, such critical constructivist theory helps individuals place themselves and their worldviews within social, cultural, historical, economic and philosophical frameworks.

When such lenses are brought to education, teachers and students begin to analyze and reconstruct their "ways of being" in the social cosmos and in the institution of education. A critical social theory identifies conflicting interests and the cultural politics emerging from this competition. These cultural politics shape every dimension of schooling, from the curriculum to interpersonal relationships among different groups. Social theory helps critical constructivists identify these power dynamics in a way that allows us to work more adeptly for democratic education, social justice and new ways of being human (Hinchey, 1998; Apple, 1999; Giroux, 1997a; McLaren, 2000; Kincheloe and McLaren, 2000).

Using social theoretical frames, critical constructivist teachers understand that knowledge is always part of a larger power struggle. In light of social theoretical insights, critical constructivist teachers ask:

- Whose interests do particular knowledges serve?
- Does the knowledge in question contribute to democratic forms of education?
- Does the phrase "democratic forms of education" refer to classroom techniques or to macro-social questions concerning the health and survival of a democratic society? Or both?
- What happens when democratic pedagogies that are student centered and negotiated fail to raise macro-social democratic questions?
- Is it possible that students could contribute to the construction of curriculum and the formulation of classroom activities but develop little insight into their self-production in relation to social, cultural, political, economic and power structures?

These are never easy questions. And they must be re-asked and re-answered throughout one's career (Brosio, 2000; Butler, 1998; Carlson, 1997; Soto, 2001; Steinberg, 2001).

In this social-theory-grounded context, professionals are better equipped to engage in conversations about the role of education in the process of social change. In such a conversation, social theoretical understandings help everyone understand the ways schooling tacitly contributes to the maintenance of the status quo with its unjust power relations. With this in mind, educators bring a critical hermeneutical understanding to their work. Simply put, this term implies that we develop rigorous ways of understanding the world so we can change it in just and democratic ways. Ever since positivists applied physical science methods to social science and educational research, there has been a struggle to address those aspects of the human condition that need not just counting but understanding. The hermeneutic dimension of research attempts to appreciate this question of meaning by focusing on the interpretive aspects of the act of knowledge production. In the **instrumental rationality** of twenty-first-century education, this hermeneutic dimension is often dismissed. Understanding that all knowledge is an interpretation, a construction, a critical education places great emphasis on the hermeneutic dimension (Shaker and Kridel, 1989; Sumara, 1996; Scering, 1997; Purpel, 1999; Zuss, 1999; Steiner, Krank, McLaren and Bahruth, 2000; Geeland and Taylor, 2000).

Instrumental rationality a dimension of positivist epistemology considered by critical theorists to be one of the most oppressive features of contemporary society. Such a form of "-hyper-reason" involves an obsession with means in preference to ends. Critical theorists claim that instrumental/technical rationality is more interested in method and efficiency than in purpose. It limits its questions to "how to" instead of "why should."

Learning from the critical hermeneutic theoretical tradition, researchers and educators learn to reexamine claims to authority in knowledge production and professional expertise. No pristine interpretation exists in educational research or skill development. No methodology, social or educational theory, or discursive form can claim a privileged position that enables the production of uncontested knowledge. Educational knowledge producers must always speak/write about the world in terms of something else in the world, "in relation to. . . ." As creatures of the world, we are oriented to it in a way that prevents us from grounding our theories and perspectives outside of it. Thus, whether we like it or not, we are all destined, as interpreters and constructors, to analyze from within its boundaries and blinders. Within the limitation, however, the interpretations emerging from the hermeneutic process can still move us to new levels of understanding. With this in mind, critical constructivist educators can begin to understand educational knowledge from an angle that allows them unanticipated insights into where it came from and whose interests it serves. Here they can gain access to blue knowledge (Gallagher, 1992; Carson and Sumara, 1997; Jardine, 1998; Ellis, 1998; Mayers, 2001a, 2001b).

With this theoretical-interpretive dimension established, educators can begin to bring previously excluded knowledge forms to their work:

- African American studies
- Feminist epistemologies
- Indigenous knowledges
- Phenomenology
- Critical theory
- Semiotics
- Discourse analysis
- Psychoanalysis
- Queer theory
- Political economic studies
- Postcolonial studies
- Poststructural analysis
- The bricolage

As teachers learn these rigorous modes of analyses, they gain new competence in the production of diverse knowledges. They learn to see anew, to discern the role of values and power in knowledges originally presented as innocent. With their 3-D glasses, teachers who grasp these theoretical constructs can interpret and make meanings around the complex interaction of theory and practice. In this context everyone involved with education sees that there are diverse and conflicting ways to conceptualize any pedagogical activity. As such complexity is noted, outside experts can no longer provide reductionistic answers for $20,000 dollars a pop. Teachers will emancipate themselves from top-down management schemes with their obligatory canned curricula, teacher scripts and outside evaluations (Snook, 1999; Edwards, 2000; Foote and Goodson, 2001).

In this social theoretical context, critical constructivist educators confront educational psychological knowledge about learning, human development, motivation and cognition. In a positivist conception of such topics, professional education students often learn that they must organize learners in relation to rigid timetables, grade levels and age levels. If such organization is neglected, then students in particular developmental stages will not learn. When social theoretical lenses are used to examine these universal pronouncements of educational psychology, profound questions are formulated and new insights emerge. In this context teacher educators and their students gain freedom to operate within Lev Vygotsky's zone of proximal development (ZPD)—a domain where mind is seen as dynamic and active, always attempting to make meaning and profoundly unpredictable (Crebbin, 2001; Edwards, 2000).

Viewed from these social theoretical lenses, positivist educational psychology has been an "excluding" discipline that has attempted to canonize the norms of Western white males from the upper-middle and upper class. Intelligence, creativity, mental health and normality in general have been defined by narrow guidelines that exclude diverse cultural manifestations of such concepts. One standard, critical constructivists argue, has worked so far, and it is the obligation of the guardians of the discipline to preserve that standard from the multicultural barbarians at the gate. What is obvious to many is that the standards and guidelines delineated by the discipline are ones best met by the guardians themselves.

The U.S. is a Eurocentric country by necessity, gatekeepers such as E. D. Hirsch maintain. So blatantly do Hirsch and his compadres erase the role of non-Europeans in American life and scholarship, one wonders how such scholars convinced themselves that the culture is devoid of African, Asian, and Native American influences. Toni Morrison (1993) refers to these absences as so "ornate" they demand our attention. Even those who have understood the impact of history and culture in shaping psychological functions could not escape the broader gravitational pull of Eurocentrism. Though Vygotsky opened an extremely important psychological conversation about the intersection of culture and mind, even he assumed the superiority of European cultural tools and forms of mental functioning to those of other cultures. Social theorists point out that such Eurocentrism, when combined with the recovery of white supremacy over the last couple of decades and the growing disparity of wealth it exacerbates, points to an epistemological crisis of knowledge and educational purpose.

This crisis, critical constructivist educators maintain, specifically involves the way we produce/construct knowledge in the positivist paradigm. In this positivist framework, educational and psychological researchers have often focused exclusively on the macro-level, ignoring the social differences that reside at the micro-level, the domain of the particular. Positivist psychology has often assumed that what is statistically most common is, accordingly, most significant. Critical constructivism seeks out the marginal, the subordinate and the "deviant," in the process gleaning insights that demand the reconfiguration of the field, the reconceptualization of common assumptions.

In this context the center-margin hierarchies so common to psychology begin to break down. The new psychology forces disciplinary change in light of the exposure of the race, class, gender and sexual construction of basic psychological concepts, in the process revealing the ways the field has served to disempower subordinate groups. At the core of the epistemological crisis is positivist psychology's inability to deal with diversity. This deficiency takes on exaggerated importance in a twenty-first century America that grows more ethnically diverse every day (King and Mitchell, 1995; Sedgwick, 1995; Wertsch and Tulviste, 1992; Fiske, 1994; Kincheloe, Steinberg and Gresson, 1996; Hicks, 1999; Soto, 2000).

Diverse Ways of Seeing: The New Multilogical Terrain of Critical Constructivism

Developing new frames of reference that move us from positivistic monological ways of seeing to diverse multilogical lenses is a central dimension of critical constructivism. The recognition of diverse frames of reference brings us to a conceptual watershed in the conversation about research and education. It is in this context that objectivist educational leaders and their allies who advocate evidence-based educational research and top-down content standards argue that critical constructivists are arguing an "anything goes" type of research and pedagogy. This is not only a duplicitous and incorrect assertion but a dangerous one as well. Understanding different modes of evaluating what constitutes high-quality academic expression is similar to Howard Gardner's recognition of multiple forms of intelligence, anthropologists' view of multiple models of social/cultural organization, the art world's appreciation of various artistic schools and different cultures' amazing modes of artistic production, and a musicologist's appreciation of the wonder of the differences in European, African and Asian forms of music.

Embracing these types of diversities does not undermine artistic or musical quality—it profoundly enhances excellence in these domains. By understanding diverse expressions, we become better artists, better musicians and better scholars. On one level the point is so obvious that it would seem unnecessary to make until we examine the monocultural, xenophobic standard content that passes for contemporary right-wing standards-driven curriculum. Such monological, defensive curricula emerge from a deep-seated sense of cultural inferiority. They find their origins in a cultural fear that the vandals must be excluded from the democratic process of negotiation. If they are not held at bay, then their cultures will overwhelm "our" own, and "we" will no longer be the chosen people, the bearers of *civilization.* Indeed, one cannot understand the history of the last third of the twentieth and the first decade of the twenty-first centuries without grasping these dynamics. The "culture wars" that shape social, political, and educational institutions in the U.S. strike at the very core of American identity and the nature of our relationship to the rest of the world in the globalized twenty-first century.

As critical constructivists help scholars escape the entrapment of these Eurocentric, reductionistic, positivistic ways of constructing self and world, teachers and researchers come to value and thus pursue new frames of reference in regard to their students, their inquiry, their classrooms and the purposes of their labor. Teachers in this context begin to look at their lessons from the perspectives of their often-marginalized students—their black students, their Latino students, their Asian students, their Native American students, and their socio-economically poor students. They examine their teaching from the vantage points of their colleagues, an outside lay-observer from the local community, or onlookers from different communities and cultures. Thus, they figuratively step out of their teacher bodies, looking down on themselves and their students as outsiders. As they hover in the epistemological ether above themselves, they examine their own education, the role of the guardians of Eurocentric reductionism in their own consciousness construction, and the ways their experiences and identity relate to these dynamics.

For example, think about what a teacher and a researcher (or a teacher-researcher) can learn about the nature of positivistic content simply by a quick look at Hopi linguistics. An examination of diverse linguistic and epistemological patterns highlights the taken-for-granted assumptions of English language speakers. Indo-European languages, for example, confine us to particular ways of thinking. They often fragment experience by devaluing context and relationship. Because of their subject-predicate matrix, these languages induce us to consider the world in terms of linear cause effect. Trapped in a view of language as a neutral medium of communication, objectivist analysts have found it hard to talk (or think) about subjects such as quantum physics, the nature of consciousness, higher orders of cognition, autopoiesis or any other concept without identifiable boundaries, specific beginnings and endings and a clear delineation of "then" and "now."

Complexity theory attempts to denaturalize the positivist, Eurocentric universalization of Indo-

European linguistics. Pointing to the fact that events in nature often have simultaneous multiple causes, many scholars argue that not all languages have difficulty with non-linearity. The Hopi and the Chinese, for example, speak "nonlinearly." Westerners from ancient Greece to the modern U.S. say "the light flashed," even if the light and the flash are inseparable. If we spoke Hopi, we would simply say, "Reh-pi," meaning "flash" (Ferguson, 1980). No linearity, no cause or effect, is implied. The complexity embraced by critical constructivism offers an alternative to reductionistic positivism, a starting place in our attempt to formulate new forms of scholarly rigor—forms that allow us to see what is currently eclipsed by the Cartesian moon. It is important to emphasize in this context that such an epistemological move to critical constructivist complexity does not mean that we throw out everything associated with modernist Cartesian-Newtonian-Baconian ways of seeing—that would be absurd. It does mean that we examine the shortcomings and strengths of such ways of constructing reality and the knowledges they have produced from diverse vantage points. Such a reconceptualization and assessment are long overdue.

The New Terrain as a Domain of Difference

Critical constructivists, as we by now know, understand that knowledge producers, curriculum developers, teachers and students perceive the world from a center located within themselves, shaped by the social and cultural context in which they operate, and framed by languages and discourses that contain within them tacit views of the world. As they dig deeper into the contexts surrounding the construction of knowledge and education, analysts sensitive to the complexity of critical constructivism find that students from different racial, ethnic, gender and class locations will relate to schooling in different ways. If students who operate far from the middle-class, white, English-speaking mainstream are not provided assistance by insightful teachers, they will be the victims of culturally insensitive, decontextualized and monological pedagogies. These students will not fail to meet monological standards because of some inability or lack of intelligence but because of a set of forces unleashed by their relation to what is often labeled the "common culture." The more positivist political and educational leaders use the term "common culture" in an unexamined way, the more those students who fall outside of its boundaries will fail.

Educators who understand contextual complexity appreciate the notion that American culture is not a homogeneous way of life but a domain of difference shaped by unequal power relations. They understand that social and educational analysts and professional practitioners must act on an appreciation of the way these differences shape people's relationships to various institutions, education in particular. If everyone is seen as a part of some narrow articulation of a common culture, then those who don't fit the mainstream criteria will find themselves looking into the society's institutions as unworthy outsiders. Critical constructivists understand these important social tendencies and make sure that steps are taken to include everyone in a diverse, democratic, high-quality education (Apple, 1996; Kincheloe and Steinberg, 1997).

The way these factors play out in the everyday life of school is multidimensional, complex, and always significant. When classroom instruction is driven by positivistic standards with their fragmented factoids, the same pedagogical actions take place repeatedly without regard for who succeeds and who fails—in particular, what social groups succeed or fail over time. A creative way of merely *delivering* content, no matter how ingenious it may be, still works to produce much the same results as long as the epistemological assumptions are the same. Thus, to avoid falling into these age-old traps, critical constructivist teachers must understand both the social context that shapes learners and the epistemological context that molds the way knowledge is constructed and educational goals are forged in the classroom. Such contextual awareness provides teachers with a monitoring system that allows them a cognizance of the multidimensional effects of their pedagogy. Of course, American education didn't need contemporary standardized content standards reforms to fall into the trap of delivering a decontextualized standardized body of unproblematized data to diverse students with long-term predictable patterns of success and failure.

For generations many teachers taught or were forced to teach *de facto* content standards by teaching the subject matter of market-driven textbooks. Questions concerning the writing and production of the textbooks were generally not asked. Thus, teachers teaching a rigorous critical constructivist curriculum have to be reflective professionals who bring an awareness of multiple contexts to the teaching act. Insights derived in this contextualizing activity allow teachers to engage in and share with students the higher-order cognitive activity of reframing knowledge and skills, of understanding the forces at work in the knowledge construction process. The reframing process moves such teachers to ask questions of belief and value: Do we believe what this author is telling us about the meaning of the short story? Do we see this description of Western expansion in the nineteenth century as a balanced account of the process? Is this a comprehensive depiction of Darwin's theory of relativity? Are the data presented in the chapter on quadratic equations worth knowing at this point in our study of math? Why is quantum mechanics not included in our physics textbook?

The ability to employ contextualization in the pursuit of multiple perspectives is an important skill of critical constructivist teachers. As students begin to see the multiple perspectives that always surround any topic, they examine such viewpoints in relation to one another (Elmore, 1997). The insights derived from such an activity lead directly to cognitive growth and an appreciation of the complexity of the cosmos. When standardized curricula are implemented on the national or the state level, the ability of critical constructivist teachers to take the multiple contexts of schooling and its students into account is undermined. Their capacity to study the context in which knowledge is constructed and validated is subverted. In such a simplified-standards-based, classroom, it doesn't matter who students are or what their specific needs may be—the curriculum has already been mandated. It doesn't matter who produced the information covered or the contextual conditions of its construction—the point is to commit it to memory. This is an insult to rigorous notions of scholarship and to the diversity of the global, not to mention the national, social landscape.

Point 12: Critical constructivists value subjugated knowledge. Utilizing the concept of the "blues idiom," we attempt to expand the concept of subjugated knowledge by drawing upon African American cultural knowledges. The result is a form of subjugated epistemology called blue knowledge.

In this portion of our discussion of critical constructivism I draw upon the aesthetic work of literary critic and blues scholar, Albert Murray (1996), to develop a concept of blue knowledge or blue epistemology. Because the blues are such an emotional, contextually specific, non-rational idiom, efforts to define them often come across as stilted and irrelevant. With that caveat in mind the blues generally involve a musical and lyrical form where the music tends to be organized around a sequence of improvised choruses played over a specific but flexible framework of rhythm and chords. Lyrically, the blues project a confrontation of life's raw existential realities such as relationships between men and women, employers and employees, or humans and nature. Though they refuse to run from the hardships of life, the lyrics of the blues are ultimately a celebration of human agency, the ability of groups and individuals to persist despite the obstacles thrown in their way. In the midst of this pain, the blues insist, we can celebrate, have a good time, and even get down. That impassioned spirit has appealed to me and shaped my life since I first comprehended it. It certainly resonates with and extends my conception of critical constructivism.

Albert Murray contends that this blues idiom is a discursive strategy that can be applied to a variety of contexts—art, literature and politics, for example. Taking Murray's cue, I am applying it here to the acts of knowledge production and pedagogy—in particular the extension of critical constructivism's multilogical epistemology of subjugated knowledges. The blues idiom in this critical constructivist context helps us appreciate the power of difference, subjugated knowledges and the importance of the view from below. Such a concept attunes knowledge producers and pedagogues to constructions of the world from which they have been shielded by their privileged location in the web of reality. Such constructions grant us new insights into the way the world operates. Often throughout my career as a teacher and researcher, individuals have asked me after a class or a speech: "Where did you get your perspective? I'd never thought of schools like that before." My reply has been that I listened carefully to those who suffered because of their experience in schools. I can see these dimensions of education, I tell them, because I have friends in low places. Many critical scholars are too busy saving the world to listen to and learn from such sources. Critical constructivists must understand the world and the nature of oppression in order to change it.

The blues aesthetic is the polar opposite of the concept of kitsch. Kitsch is the aesthetic orientation that denies the existence of shit in the world. In other words it retreats from confronting the rawest and most troubling dimensions of human existence. The blues aesthetic works to keep the blues away in the very act of acknowledging that there is good reason for particular individuals to have the blues. The blues are never in denial. Indeed, the blues aesthetic is constructed in the midst of injustice and is the essence of a subjugated knowledge. Yet in the middle of this injustice and the despair it drags along with it, the blues aesthetic promotes a form of play. While, of course, many other strategies against oppression are necessary, this play in the shadow of despair is a powerful assertion of emancipation. This affirmative blues dynamic grants one the agency to face pain, injustice and tragedy with a tragic magic, with a sense of style and dignity. Such an ontological poetry creates a sense of possibility that holds implications for critical constructivists as they produce knowledge and teach their classes.

The aesthetic of affirmation, of lament wrapped in celebration constructed by the blues, finds expression in cultures other than African American. In Spanish culture and the gypsy subculture, flamenco music expresses a similar power as singers squeeze out wails that combine the sound of Muslim calls to prayer with the energy and melody of soul men and women. In Southern Appalachian Mountain bluegrass we also witness dimensions of the blues aesthetic as listeners and performers whoop and holler for joy. In the blues aesthetic, *jouissance* is power. As Albert Murray (1996) puts it:

> The verbal response to a blues vamp, whether in a ramshackle honky-tonk or a swanky midtown New York nightspot, is not "alas" or "alack" but rather some expression equivalent to "hey now" or Yeah now" or "Lord, am I born to die." At such a time "Lord, have mercy" means "Lord, enable me to endure the good time that this music is already generating" (p. 203).

Murray provides great insight into the power of the blues idiom and the symbolism of particular performers in social and political context. Writing about Louis Armstrong's trumpet in the 1930s and 1940s, Murray argues that it signified a spirit of exploration and readjustment in the lives of urban African Americans testing what society would allow of them in this period. Taking a cue from Murray, one can extend his concern with the symbolic dimensions of the blues men and women following Armstrong. For example, Muddy Waters' deployment of the blues in the mid-1950s in his songs and guitar work resonated well with the worldwide rebellion of colonized peoples against centuries of Euro-colonialism and the American expression of the anti-colonial impulse in the civil rights movement.

In his famous song "Mannish Boy," Waters puts

forward a heroic articulation of the blues aesthetic with a swaggering assertion of black manhood in the midst of white resistance to social change. When accompanied by one of the most famous and hard-driving blues riffs of all time played through amplified electric instruments atop a relentless and stomping beat, one can understand the meaning of subjugated knowledges as dangerous information. Unafraid to project confidence and even, God forbid, black male sexuality, Waters' blues screamed "I'm a Man" in a epoch where that simple assertion was rejected by a large segment of the white population.

Add to Waters' signification the symbolism of Aretha Franklin's powerful assertion of black womanhood in her blues and soul work in the 1960s, and a new dimension of the African American blues aesthetic is unleashed. When Franklin sang "Respect" in 1967, it was not a plea for dignity but rather a demand in the spirit of Rap Brown's proclamations of Black Power in the same year. Indeed, Aretha Franklin was singing not only to black men but to the world at large to reject stereotyped racial and gender roles and give black women just a little respect. The world must change so that we can enter into new egalitarian and eroticized relationships where we can "sock it to" one another. If you want what I got, Franklin maintained, you better adopt a new conception of manhood. In the spirit of the blues aesthetic, Franklin acknowledges there are bad times, but just think about what we can do all night long in spite of them. A feminist curriculum of possibility is constructed in Franklin's blue knowledge.

And then there was Jimi Hendrix. Hendrix drew upon the blues as the basis for a psychedelic rock that never lost touch with celebration in the midst of despair. His guitar so often reflected in its distortion the awareness of the anti-colonial fight and, in particular, the expanding backlash to the struggle that still helps shape right-wing American politics and social life in the twenty-first century. Hendrix's blues aesthetic smells of napalm in the morning as it illustrates the connection between the horrors of the Vietnam War with life in the urban streets of the U.S.

Hendrix's Woodstock rendition of "The Star Spangled Banner" features a guitar that wails and cries punctuated by the explosions, screams of the wounded, roar of war machines, and death rattles of the Indochinese jungle and African American urban life. Never far from the blues aesthetic, Hendrix's portrayal of the horror of his times elicited profound pleasure and excitement from his listeners. Lord, allow me the strength to endure the aesthetic and political power Hendrix's music generated. There is pleasure to be derived even in an era that produces widespread manic depression.

Down on Highway 61: Constructing Blue Knowledge and Blue Cognition

Armstrong, Waters, Franklin and Hendrix are just a few of the countless blues artists that could be brought into our discussion of blue knowledge. In the contemporary era, many rap artists create similar aesthetic statements, albeit styled for a new era and new realities. Blue knowledge is always subjective and complex, grounded in ambiguity and intersecting narratives of tragedy, comedy, melodrama and irony. Just as classical musicologists relegated the blues to a low rung on the aesthetic ladder, positivist scientists and the elite arbiters of quality scholarship often categorize blue knowledge as soft data or unvalidated speculation. Blue knowledge reflects critical constructivism's concern with power and oppression and the ways that human beings are exploited and degraded by these forces. Concurrently, blue knowledge extends critical constructivism's concern with confronting nihilistic determinism, celebrating human agency, and the creation of a pedagogy of possibility in spite of the forces aligned against such cultural and academic work.

Hell, blue knowledge pushes scholars to laugh, to be ironic, to embrace a humble stance, regardless of the institutional pressures operating to suppress such irreverent *jouissance*. Despite the protestations of the puritans of the right and the left, critical constructivist advocates of blue knowledge seriously study oppression but are always ready to celebrate manifestations of the genius and magnificence of those who find themselves in such dire circumstances. Moreover, critical constructivists are sufficiently humble to learn from the blue knowledges of the exploited. They learn not only about institutions from those who have suffered as a result of their existence but they learn from various manifestations of the blues aesthetic. They learn from the power of improvisation and the high order of cognitive ability it demands. They learn to rock, swing, roll through the world—such orientations hold profound implications for our concept of a critical ontology developed earlier in the book.

Thus, to produce blue knowledge, critical constructivists must possess a rigorous understanding of mainstream knowledges, epistemologies and methodologies. We must understand the ways they shape the ways we construct our views of the world as well as ourselves and others. Then we must study carefully subjugated forms of knowledges, epistemologies and methodologies and figure out how to use them in conjunction with other ways of seeing in order to gain a more textured and sensitive view of the world. Taking yet another example from the blues musical form, consider the notion of the "break" where the singer does not sing or the band does not play the established lead melody to make way for an improvised instrumental "fill" or "vamp." It is in the break where the individual musician has his or her opportunity to "show their stuff," to bring down the house. The break provides an opportunity for heroism as guitarists, pianists, horn players, harmonica players, etc., show their "grace under pressure, creativity in an emergency, continuity in the face of disjuncture" (Murray, 1996, p. 95).

Thus, improvisational ability is central to the blues aesthetic. It is fascinating to examine this dynamic in a cognitive context, for some of the most sophisticated articulations of contemporary cognitive theory—socio-cognition and enactivism—reach the same conclusion. Thus, the African American blues aesthetic was aware of a key aspect of higher orders of thinking completely missed by mainstream cognitive psychology throughout the twentieth century and, for that matter, the early twenty-first century as well. Enactivists, for example, understand that the problems of the physical, social, psychological and educational domains rarely present themselves in a well-structured, puzzle-like way.

Rationalistic technical thinking does not work very well when it confronts lived world problems that are complex and ill structured. Such situations demand more than procedural, technical reasoning. Analysts—not unlike blues musicians improvising in the break—have to understand a range of tacit knowledges, the multiple contexts in which a problem is situated, and thinking processes that may or may not be of value. Critical constructivist students of cognition make an important breakthrough in this context. They understand that the step-by-step procedures laid down by rationalists and the rules of rigorous research specified by positivists can hinder rather than help in the complications of the lived world. Enactivists maintain that such rules must melt away in the specificity and improvisation of immediate experience. As argued in Chapter 2, we use knowledges as we figure out their meanings and deploy them in the demands of specific situations.

This is why enactivism is so important in critical constructivism. As we teach about the workings of power and the construction of the individual, it is one thing to *theorize* about these complicated dynamics. Just as the enactivists argue, it is quite different to *enact* these ideas in the immediate action of everyday life. Blue cognition embraces the notion of crazy wisdom, the immediate coping abilities, the improvisational finesse to incorporate an understanding of power and the cultivation of human agency in relation to it. This concept is a central dimension of critical constructivism's attempt to develop a complex way of constructing knowledge and making meaning that can change the tenor of educational goals and pedagogical practices. Teachers who possess these abilities are great producers of abstract knowledge and theory—and this dimension is indispensable. They also have the ability to enact such knowledges into lived practices and everyday situations. Indeed, they find it problematic to separate the constructivist dimension of knowledge production from its enactment in the complexities of the world. They hold a reflective awareness of when their actions contradict the knowledges and the larger principles of critical constructivist systems of meaning.

Thus, critical constructivism's blue knowledge and blue cognition induce us to develop new ways to address complex, contextually embedded problems rather than to retreat to the decontextualized abstractions of positivism. In this zone of blue we look not simply at things-in-themselves but the relationships among phenomena and the patterns these relationships create. Here rests a key dimension to the creative process, the activity that transforms raw experience into a complex and evocative aesthetic construct (Murray, 1996). Here critical constructivists seek form in chaos, a quest that shapes the nature and even the quality of human existence. Without our blue knowledge and cognition we fall into the trap of positivism. Such a trap is characterized by the belief that objectivist science has more to tell us about human behavior than any other form of knowledge production.

In this context we become trapped in objectivism's certainty about the stimulus and response dynamics of human beings. Such certainty leads us to develop standardized curricula and scripted lessons for teachers because we have scientific proof of how students learn. Such universal knowledge in its failure to account for context, specificity and the complexity of human interaction produces tragic consequences for those who fall outside the boundaries of "normality."

Such knowledge dehumanizes people as it values:

- statistics over insight
- step-by-step procedures in teaching over the

crazy wisdom of informed improvisation

- machine-like predictability of human behaviour over a contextualized understanding of the rich ambiguity of human action.

In the best tradition of blue knowledge, Albert Murray (1996) writes about that which positivism fails to discern.

> Human beings . . . unlike machines may give high-octane performance on low-octane fuel in the world. Deprived machines always gasp in desperation and run down; deprived human beings, on the other hand, may become immensely creative (p. 208).

Thus, in blue knowledge, critical constructivists pursue their quest for rigorous, humane and democratic knowledges and ways of constructing knowledges. It is important to note that blue knowledges and blue cognitive styles are sought out not simply in the pursuit of diversity. They are sought out primarily because they are so smart, because they give us ideas about how we can become smarter, more humble and more just in our interactions in the world. While there are many exciting dimensions to critical constructivism, the one that engages me the most is its sense of the "not yet." Critical constructivist research and education really are sites of possibility that challenge our imagination about what could be. In this spirit, critical constructivists assert that you ain't seen nothing yet.

Glossary

Instrumental rationality—a dimension of positivist epistemology considered by critical theorists to be one of the most oppressive features of contemporary society. Such a form of "hyper-reason" involves an obsession with means in preference to ends. Critical theorists claim that instrumental/technical rationality is more interested in method and efficiency than in purpose. It limits its questions to "how to" instead of "why should."

References and Resources

Agger, B. (1992). *The Discourse of Domination: From the Frankfurt School to Postmodernism.* Evanston, IL: Northwestern University Press.

Allen, M. (2000). Voice of Reason http://www.curtin.edu.au/learn/unit/10846/arrow/vorall.htm

Apple, M. (1996). Dominance and Dependency: Situating *The Bell Curve* within the Conservative Restoration. In J. Kincheloe, S. Steinberg and A. Gresson (Eds.), *Measured Lies: The Bell Curve Examined.* New York: St. Martin's.

Apple, M. (1999). *Power, Meaning, and Identity: Essays in Critical Educational Studies.* New York: Peter Lang.

Arlin, P. (1975). Cognitive Development in Adulthood: A Fifth Stage? *Developmental Psychology,* **11**,5, pp. 602–6.

Aronowitz, S. (1988). *Science as Power: Discourse and Ideology in Modern Society.* Minneapolis: University of Minnesota Press.

Aronowitz, S. (1996). The Politics of Science Wars. In A. Ross (Ed.), *Science Wars.* Durham, NC: Duke University Press.

Aronowitz, S. and H. Giroux (1991). *Post-modern Education: Politics, Culture, and Social Criticism.* Minneapolis: University of Minnesota Press.

Barton, A. and M. Osborne (Eds.) (2001). *Teaching Science in Diverse Settings: Marginalized Discourses and Classroom Practices*. New York: Peter Lang.

Benson, G. (1989). Epistemology and the Science Curriculum. *Journal of Curriculum Studies,* **21**, 4, pp. 329–44.

Besag, F. (1986). Reality and Research. *American Behavioral Scientist,* **30**,1, pp. pp. 6–14.

Bloom, A. (1987). *The Closing of the American Mind.* New York: Simon and Schuster.

Bohm, D. and M. Edwards (1991). *Changing Consciousness*. San Francisco: Harper.

Bohm, D. and F. Peat (1987). *Science, Order, and Creativity*. New York: Bantam.

Bowers, C. and D. Flinders (1990). *Responsive Teaching: An Ecological Approach to Classroom Patterns of Language, Culture, and Thought.* New York: Teachers College Press.

Bracy, G. (1987). Measurement-driven Instruction: Catchy Phrase, Dangerous Practice. *Phi Delta Kappan,* **68**, 9, pp. 683–86.

Briggs, J. and F. Peat (1989). *Turbulent Mirror.* New York: Harper and Row.

Britzman, D. (1991). *Practice Makes Practice: A Critical Study of Learning to Teach.* Albany: State University of New York Press.

Brooks, M. (1984). A Constructivist Approach to Staff Development. *Educational Leadership*, **32**, pp. 23–27.

Brosio, R. (1994). *A Radical Democratic Critique of Capitalist Education*. New York: Peter Lang.

Brosio, R. (2000). *Philosophical Scaffolding for the Construction of Critical Democratic Education*. New York: Peter Lang.

Brown, C. and J. Davis (2000). *Black Sons to Mothers: Compliments, Critiques, and Challenges for Cultural Workers in Education*. New York: Peter Lang.

Brown, R. (1993). Cultural Representation and Ideological Domination, *Social Forces*, **71**, 3, pp. 657–76.

Brown, R. (1994). Rhetoric, Textuality, and the Postmodern Turn in Sociological Theory. In S. Seidman (Ed.), *The Postmodern Turn: New Perspectives in Social Theory*. New York: Cambridge University Press.

Brown, S. (2001). *Reconstructing School Mathematics: Problems with Problems and the Real World*. New York: Peter Lang.

Bruner, J. (1996). *The Culture of Education*. Cambridge, MA: Harvard University Press.

Burbules, N. and R. Beck (1999). Critical Thinking and Critical Pedagogy: Relations, Differences, and Limits. In T. Popkewitz and L. Fendler (Eds.) *Critical Theories in Education*. New York: Routledge.

Butler, M. (1998). Negotiating Place: The Importance of Children's Realities. In J. Kincheloe and S. Steinberg (Eds.), *Students as Researchers: Creating Classrooms That Matter*. London: Falmer.

Bybee, C. (2004). Kids and the News. In S. Steinberg and J. Kincheloe (Eds.), *Kinderculture: The Corporate Construction of Childhood*. 2nd Ed. Boulder, CO: Westview.

Capra, F. (1996). *The Web of Life: A New Scientific Understanding of Living Systems*. New York: Anchor.

Carlson, D. (1997). *Making Progress: Education and Culture in New Times*. New York: Teachers College Press.

Carlson, D. and M. Apple (Eds.) (1998). *Power/Knowledge/ Pedagogy: The Meaning of Democratic Education in Unsettling Times*. Boulder, CO: Westview.

Carson, T. and D. Sumara (1997). *Action Research as a Living Practice*. New York: Peter Lang.

Carter, R. (2004). Visual Literacy: Critical Thinking with the Visual Image. In D. Weil and J. Kincheloe (Eds.). *Critical Thinking and Learning: An Encyclopedia*. Westport, CT: Greenwood.

Cary, R. (1998). *Critical Art Pedagogy: Foundations for Postmodern Art Education*. New York: Garland.

Cary, R. (2004). Art and Aesthetics. In D. Weil and J. Kincheloe (Eds.) *Critical Thinking and Learning: An Encyclopedia*. Westport, CT: Greenwood.

Chiari, G. and M. Nuzzo (1993). Personal Construct Theory within Psychological Constructivism: Precursor or Avant-Garde? http://www.cesipc.it/materali/epistandermconstructivism.pdf

Coben, D. (1998). *Radical Heroes: Gramsci, Freire and the Politics of Adult Education*. New York: Garland.

Cochran-Smith, M. (2000). The Outcomes Question in Teacher Education. Paper Presented to the Annual Meeting of the American Educational Research Association, New Orleans.

Cochran-Smith, M. and S. Lytle (1993). *Inside/Outside: Teacher Research and Knowledge*. New York: Teachers College Press.

Cochran-Smith, M. and S. Lytle (1998). Teacher Research: The Question that Persists. *International Journal of Leadership in Education*, 10, pp. 19–36.

Connell, R. (1989). Curriculum Politics, Hegemony, and Strategies of Social Change. In H. Giroux and R. Simon (Eds.), *Popular Culture: Schooling and Everyday Life.* Granby, MA: Bergin and Garvey.

Crebbin, W. (2001). The Critically Reflective Practitioner. http://www.ballarat.edu.au/~wcrebbin/TB780/Critreflect.html

Degenaar, J. (1995). Myth and the Collision of Cultures. *Myth and Symbol*. 2.

Denzin, N. (1987). Postmodern Children. *Caring for Children/Society.* March/April, pp. 32–35.

Denzin, N. and Y. Lincoln (2000). *The Handbook of Qualitative Research.* 2nd Edition. Thousand Oaks, CA: Sage.

Derrida, J. (1976). *Of Grammatology.* G. Spivak, Trans. Baltimore: Johns Hopkins University Press.

Derrida, J. (1981). *Dissemination.* Trans. B. Johnson. Chicago: University of Chicago Press.

Devault, M. (1996). Talking Back to Sociolog: Distinctive Contributions of Feminist Methodologies. *Annual Review of Sociology,* 22.

Dewey, J. (1916) *Democracy and Education.* New York: The Free Press.

Doll, W. (1989). Foundations for a Post-modern Curriculum. *Journal of Curriculum Studies.* **21**, 3, pp. 243–53.

Donald, J. (1993). The Natural Man, the Virtuous Woman: Reproducing Citizens. In C. Jenks (Ed.), *Cultural Reproduction.* New York: Routledge.

Dougiamas, M. (2002). A Journey into Constructivism. Share, 4, 92. http://www.shareeducation.com.ar/past%20issues/share%2092.htm

Edwards, A. (2000). Researching Pedagogy: A Sociocultural Agenda. Inaugural Lecture, University of Birmingham. http://www.edu.bham.ac.uk/SAT/Edwards1.html

Eisner, E. (1984). Can Educational Research Inform Educational Practice? *Phi Delta Kappan,* **65**, 7, pp. 447–52.

Ellis, J. (1998). Interpretive Inquiry as Student Research. In S. Steinberg and J. Kincheloe (Eds.), *Students as Researchers: Creating Classrooms That Matter.* pp. 49–63. London: Taylor & Francis.

Elmore, R. (1997). Education Policy and Practice in the Aftermath of TIMSS. http://www.enc.org/TIMSS/addtools/pubs/symp/cd163/cd163.htm

Fee, E. (1982). Is Feminism a Threat to Scientific Objectivity? *International Journal of Women's Studies,* **4**, 4, pp. 378–92.

Fenwick, T. (2000). Experiential Learning in Adult Education: A Comparative Framework. http://www.ualberta.ca/~tfenwick/ext/aeq.htm

Ferguson, M. (1980). *The Aquarian Conspiracy: Personal and Social Transformation in Our Time*. Los Angeles: J. P. Tarcher.

Ferreira, M. and F. Alexandre (2000). Education for Citizenship: The Challenge of Teacher Education in Postmodernity. http://www.ioe.ac.uk./ccs/conference2000/papers/epsd/ferreiraandalexandre.html

Fischer, F. (1998). Beyond Empiricism: Policy Inquiry in Postpositivist Perspective. *Policy Studies Journal*, 26, 1, pp. 129–46.

Fiske, J. (1993). *Power Plays, Power Works*. New York: Verso.

Fiske, J. (1994). *Media Matters: Everyday Culture and Political Change*. Minneapolis: University of Minnesota Press.

Fontana, A. (1994). Ethnographic Trends in the Postmodern Era. In D. Dickens and A. Fontana (Eds.), *Postmodernism and Social Inquiry*. New York: Guilford.

Foote, M. and I. Goodson (2001). Regulating Teachers—A Sword over Their Heads: The Standards Movement as a Disciplinary Device. In J. Kincheloe and D. Weil (Eds.), *Standards and Schooling in the United States: An Encyclopedia*, 3 vols. Santa Barbara, CA: ABC-Clio.

Fosnot, C. (1988). The Dance of Education. Paper Presented to the Annual Conference of the Association for Educational Communication and Technology, New Orleans.

Foucault, M. (1980). *Power/Knowledge: Selected Interviews and Other Writings*. Ed. C. Gordon. New York: Pantheon.

Frankenberg, R. (1993). *White Women, Race Matters: The Social Construction of Whiteness*. Minneapolis: University of Minnesota Press.

Freire, P. (1970). *Pedagogy of the Oppressed*. New York: Herder and Herder.

Freire, P. (1985). *The Politics of Education: Culture, Power, and Liberation*. South Hadley, MA: Bergin and Garvey.

Gallagher, S. (1992). *Hermeneutics and Education*. Albany: State University of New York Press.

Geeland, D. (1996). Learning to Communicate: Developing as a Science Teacher. http://bravus.port5.com/learn.htm

Geeland, D. and P. Taylor (2000). Writing Our Lived Experience: Beyond the (Pale) Hermeneutic, *Electronic Journal of Science Education*, 5. http://unr.edu/homepage/crowther/ejse/geelanetal.html

Getzel, G. (1997). Humanizing the University: An Analysis and Recommendations. http://humanism.org/opinions/articles.html.

Giroux, H. (1997a). *Pedagogy and the Politics of Hope: Theory, Culture, and Schooling*. Boulder, CO: Westview.

Giroux, H. (1997b). Are Disney Movies Good for Your Kids? In S. Steinberg and J. Kincheloe (Eds.), *Kinderculture: The Corporate Construction of Childhood*. Boulder, CO: Westview.

Gordon, M. (2001). Philosophical Analysis and Standards—Philosophical and Analytical Standards. In J. Kincheloe and D. Weil (Eds.), *Standards and Schooling in the United States: An Encyclopedia*. 3 vols. Santa Barbara, CA: ABC-Clio.

Gordon, E., F. Miller and D. Rollock (1990). Coping with Communicentric Bias in Knowledge Production in the Social Sciences. *Educational Researcher,* **19**, 3, pp. 14–19.

Gray, H. (1995). *Watching Race: Television and the Struggle for Blackness*. Minneapolis: University of Minnesota Press.

Gresson, A. (1995). *The Recovery of Race in America*. Minneapolis: University of Minnesota Press.

Grimmett, P. (1999). Teacher Educators as Mettlesome Mermaids. *International Electronic Journal for Leadership in Learning,* **3**, 12. http://www.ucalgary.ca/~iejll

Gubrium, J. and J. Holstein (2000). Analyzing Interpretive Practice. In N. Denzin and Y. Lincoln (Eds.), *Handbook of Qualitative Research,* 2nd ed. Thousand Oaks, CA, Sage.

Harvey, D. (1989). *The Condition of Postmodernity*. Cambridge, MA: Basil Blackwell.

Hicks, E. (1999). *Ninety-five Languages and Seven Forms of Intelligence*. New York: Peter Lang.

Hinchey, P. (1998). *Finding Freedom in the Classroom: A Practical Introduction to Critical Theory.* New York: Peter Lang.

Hoban, G. and G. Erickson (1998). Frameworks for Sustaining Professional Learning. Paper Presented at the Australasian Science Education Research Association, Darwin, Australia.

Horn, R. (2000). *Teacher Talk: A Postformal Inquiry into Educational Change*. New York: Peter Lang.

Horn, R. and J. Kincheloe (Eds.) (2001). *American Standards: Quality Education in a Complex World—the Texas Case.* New York: Peter Lang.

Howley, A., E. Pendarvis and C. Howley (1993). Anti-intellectualism in U.S. Schools. *Education Policy Analysis Archives,* **1**, 6.

Jaggar, A. (1983). *Feminist Politics and Human Nature.* Totowa, NJ: Rowman and Allanheld.

Jardine, D. (1998). *To Dwell with a Boundless Heart: Essays in Curriculum Theory, Hermeneutics, and the Ecological Imagination.* New York: Peter Lang.

Karunaratne, V. (1997). Buddhism, Science, and Dialectics. http://humanism.org/opinions/articles.html

Kaufman, B. (1978). Piaget, Marx, and the Political Ideology of Schooling. *Journal of Curriculum Studies,* **10**, 1, pp. 19–44.

Kellner, D. (1990). *Television and the Crisis of Democracy.* Boulder, CO: Westview.

Kelly, G. (1955). *The Psychology of Personal Constructs.* New York: Norton.

Kincheloe, J. (1993). *Toward a Critical Politics of Teacher Thinking: Mapping the Postmodern.* Westport, CT: Bergin and Garvey.

Kincheloe, J. (1995). *Toil and Trouble: Good Work, Smart Workers, and the Integration of Academic and Vocational Education.* New York: Peter Lang.

Kincheloe, J. (1999). *How Do We Tell the Workers? The Socio-economic Foundations of Work and Vocational Education.* Boulder, CO: Westview.

Kincheloe, J. (2001). *Getting Beyond the Facts: Teaching Social Studies/Social Sciences in the Twenty-first Century.* New York: Peter Lang.

Kincheloe, J. (2002). *The Sign of the Burger: McDonald's and the Culture of Power.* Philadelphia: Temple University Press.

Kincheloe, J. (2003). *Teachers as Researchers: Qualitative Paths to Empowerment.* 2nd ed. London: Falmer.

Kincheloe, J. (2004). *Critical Pedagogy.* New York: Peter Lang.

Kincheloe, J. and K. Berry (2004). *Rigor and Complexity in Educational Research: Conceptualizing the Bricolage.* London: Open University Press.

Kincheloe, J. and P. McLaren (2000). Rethinking Critical Theory and Qualitative Research. In N. Denzin and Y. Lincoln (Eds.), *Handbook of Qualitative Research.* Thousand Oaks, CA: Sage.

Kincheloe, J. and S. Steinberg (1993). A Tentative Description of Post-formal Thinking: The Critical Confrontation with Cognitive Theory. *Harvard Educational Review,* **63**, 3, pp. 296–320.

Kincheloe, J. and S. Steinberg (1997). *Changing Multiculturalism.* London: Open University Press.

Kincheloe, J. and S. Steinberg (2004). *The Miseducation of the West: How Schools and the Media Distort our Understanding of the Islamic World*. Westport, CT: Greenwood.

Kincheloe, J. and D. Weil (Eds.) (2001). *Standards and Schooling in the U.S.: An Encyclopedia*. 3 vols. Santa Barbara, CA: ABC-Clio.

Kincheloe, J., S. Steinberg and A. Gresson (Eds.) (1996). *Measured Lies: The Bell Curve Examined*. New York: St. Martin's.

Kincheloe, J., S. Steinberg and P. Hinchey (1999). *The Postformal Reader: Cognition and Education*. New York: Falmer.

Kincheloe, J., S. Steinberg, N. Rodriguez and R. Chennault (1998). *White Reign: Deploying Whiteness in America*. New York: St. Martin's.

Kincheloe, J., S. Steinberg and D. Tippins (1999). *The Stigma of Genius: Einstein, Consciousness, and Education*. New York: Peter Lang.

Kincheloe, J., S. Steinberg and L. Villaverde (Eds.) (1999). *Rethinking Intelligence: Confronting Psychological Assumptions about Teaching and Learning*. New York: Routledge.

King, J. and C. Mitchell (1995). *Black Mothers to Sons*. New York: Peter Lang.

Knobel, M. (1999) *Everyday Literacies: Students, Discourse, and Social Practice*. New York: Peter Lang.

Kramer, D. (1983). Post-formal Operations? A Need for Further Conceptualization. *Human Development, 26*, pp. 91–105.

Kroath, F. (1989). How Do Teachers Change Their Practical Theories? *Cambridge Journal of Education,* **19**, 1, pp. 59–69.

Lather, P. (1991). *Getting Smart: Feminist Research and Pedagogy with/in the Postmodern*. New York: Routledge.

Lather, P. (1993). Fertile Obsession: Validity after Poststructuralism. *Sociological Quarterly*, 34, pp. 673–93.

Lave, J. and E. Wenger (1991). *Situated Learning: Legitimate Peripheral Participation*. New York: Cambridge University Press.

Lavine, T. (1984). *From Socrates to Sartre: The Philosophic Quest*. New York: Bantam Books.

Lemke, J. (1993). Discourse, Dynamics, and Social Change. *Cultural Dynamics, 6,* pp. 243–275.

Lemke, J. (1995). *Textual Politics: Discourse and Social Dynamics*. London: Taylor & Francis.

Leonardo, Z. (2004). Ideology and Critical Thinking. In D. Weil and J. Kincheloe (Eds.) *Critical Thinking and Learning: An Encyclopedia.* Westport, CT: Greenwood.

Lepani, B. (1998). Creating Learning Communities. http://www.oten.edu.au/qltech/ite/df/learndoc.pdf

Lester, S. (2001). Learning for the Twenty-First Century. In J. Kincheloe and D. Weil (Eds.) *Standards and Schooling in the U.S.: An Encyclopedia.* 3 vols. Santa Barbara, CA: ABC-Clio.

Lincoln, Y. and E. Guba (1985). *Naturalistic Inquiry.* Beverly Hills, CA: Sage.

Lovelock, J. and Margulis, L. (1974).. Homeostatic Tendencies of the Earth's Atmosphere. *Origins of Life,* 5, pp. 12–22.

Lowe, D. (1982). *History of Bourgeois Perception.* Chicago: University of Chicago Press.

Luke, T. (1991). Touring Hyperreality: Critical Theory Confronts Informational Society. In P. Wexler (Ed.), *Critical Theory Now* (pp. 1–26). New York: Falmer.

Lutz, K., K. Jones and J. Kendall (1997). Expanding the Praxis Debate: Contributions to Clinical Inquiry. *Advances in Nursing Science,* **20**, 2.

Macedo, D. (1994). *Literacies of Power: What Americans Are Not Allowed to Know.* Boulder, CO: Westview.

Madison, G. (1988). *The Hermeneutics of Postmodernity: Figures and Themes.* Bloomington, IN: Indiana University Press.

Malewski, E. (2001a) "Administration—Administrative Leadership and Public Consciousness: Discourse Matters in the Struggle for New Standards," in J. Kincheloe and D. Weil (Eds.), *Standards and Schooling in the United States: An Encyclopedia.* 3 vols. Santa Barbara, CA: ABC-Clio.

Malewski, E. (2001b). Queer Sexuality—The Trouble with Knowing: Standards of Complexity and Sexual Orientations. In J. Kincheloe and D. Weil (Eds.) *Standards and Schooling in the U.S.: An Encyclopedia.* 3 vols. Santa Barbara, CA: ABC-Clio.

Marijuan, P. (1994). Information Revisited. Paper Presented to the First Conference on the Foundations of Information Science, Madrid, Spain.

Marzano, R. and J. Kendall (1999). The Fall and Rise of Standards-Based Education. http://www.mcrel.org/standards/articles/fall-and-rise-one.dsp

Matthews, M. (2003). Constructivism in Science and Mathematics Education. http://wwwcsi.unian.it/educa/inglese/matthews.html

Maturana, H. and F. Varela (1980). *Autopoiesis and Cognition: The Realization of the Living*. Boston: Reidel.

Maturana, H. and F. Varela (1987). *The Tree of Knowledge*. Boston: Shambhala.

Mayers, M. (2001a). Interpretation—Hermeneutics, Invitation to Meaning Making: The Ecology of a Complexity of Standards, Educational Research, Policy, and Praxis. In J. Kincheloe and D. Weil (Eds.). *Standards and Schooling in the United States: An Encyclopedia*. 3 vols. Santa Barbara, CA: ABC-Clio.

Mayers, M. (2001b). *Street Kids and Streetscapes: Panhandling, Politics, and Prophecies*. New York: Peter Lang.

Mayers, M. and J. Field (2004). Critical Hermeneutics in the Classroom. In D. Weil and J. Kincheloe (Eds.) *Critical Thinking and Learning: An Encyclopedia*. Westport, CT: Greenwood.

McGinty, S. (Ed.) (2001). *The Politics and Machinations of Educational Research: International Case Studies*. New York: Peter Lang.

McLaren, P. (1989). *Life in Schools. New York:* Longman.

McLaren, P. (1995). *Critical Pedagogy and Predatory Culture: Oppositional Politics in a Postmodern Era*. New York: Routledge.

McLaren, P. (2000). *Che Guevara, Paulo Freire, and the Pedagogy of Revolution*. Lanham, MD: Rowman and Littlefield.

McLaren et al. (1995). *Rethinking Media Literacy: A Critical Pedagogy of Representation*. New York: Peter Lang.

Mies, M. (1982). Toward a Methodology for Feminist Research. In G. Bowles and R. Klein (Eds.), *Theories of Women's Studies*. Boston: Routledge and Kegan Paul.

Morrison, T. (1993). *Playing in the Dark: Whiteness and the Literary Imagination*. New York: Vintage.

Murphie, A. (1998). Cyberfictions and Hypertext: What Is Happening to Text? http://wwwmcs.elm.mq.edu.au/staff/Andrew/307/hypeprt.html

Murray, A. (1996). *The Blue Devils of Nada: A Contemporary American Approach to Aesthetic Statement*. New York: Vintage.

Musolf, R. (1992). Structure, Institutions, Power and Ideology: New Directions within Symbolic Interactionism, *The Sociological Quarterly*, **33**, 2, pp. 171–89.

Newland, P. (1997). Logical Types of Learning. http://www.envf.port.ac.uk/newmedia/lecturenotes/EMMA/at2n.htm

Noblit, G. (1984). The Prospects of an Applied Ethnography for Education: A Sociology of Knowledge Interpretation. *Educational Evaluation and Policy Analysis*, **6**, 1, pp. 95–101.

Noblit, G. (1999). *Particularities: Collected Essays on Ethnography and Education*. New York: Peter Lang.

Ohanian, S. (1999). *One Size Fits Few: The Folly of Educational Standards*. Portsmouth, NH: Heinemann.

O'Riley, P. (2003). *Technology, Culture, and Socioeconomics: A Rhizoanalysis of Educational Discourses*. New York: Peter Lang.

O'Sullivan, E. (1999). *Transformative Learning: Educational Vision for the Twenty-first Century*. New York: Zed.

Owen, D. and M. Doerr (1999). *None of the Above: The Truth behind the SATs*. Lanham, MD: Rowman and Littlefield.

Pang, V., G. Gay and W. Stanley (1995). Expanding Conceptions of Community and Civic Competencies for a Multicultural Society. *Theory and Research in Social Education*, **23**, 4, pp. 302–31.

Paulson, R. (1995). Mapping Knowledge Perspectives in Studies of Educational Change. In P. Cookson, Jr. and B. Schneider (Eds.), *Transforming Schools*. New York: Garland.

Perry, P. (2001). *A Composition of Consciousness: Roads of Reflection from Freire to Elbow*. New York: Peter Lang.

Pickering, J. (1999). The Self Is a Semiotic Process. *Journal of Consciousness Studies*, **6**, 4, pp. 31–47.

Pinar, W. (1994). *Autobiography, Politics, and Sexuality: Essays in Curriculum Theory, 1972-1992*. New York: Peter Lang.

Powell, R. (2001). *Straight Talk: Growing as Multicultural Educators*. New York: Peter Lang.

Prigogine, I. and I. Stengers (1984). *Order out of Chaos*. New York: Basic Books.

Probyn, E. (1993). True Voices and Real People: The "Problem" of the Autobiographical in Cultural Studies. In V. Blundell, J. Shepard and I. Taylor (Eds.), *Relocating Cultural Studies: Developments in Theory and Research*. New York: Routledge.

Progler, Y. (2001) Social Studies—Social Studies Standards: Diversity, Conformity, Complexity. In J. Kincheloe and D. Weil (Eds.) *Standards and Schooling in the United States: An Encyclopedia*, 3 vols. Santa Barbara, CA: ABC-Clio.

Purpel, D. (1999). *Moral Outrage in Education*. New York: Peter Lang.

Rasberry, G. (2001). *Writing Research/Researching Writing: Through a Poet's I.* New York: Peter Lang.

Reason, P. and H. Bradbury (2000). Introduction: Inquiry and Participation in Search of a World Worthy of Human Aspiration. In P. Reason and H. Bradbury (Eds.), *Handbook of Action Research: Participative Inquiry and Practice.* Thousand Oaks, CA: Sage.

Richardson, F. and R. Woolfolk (1994). Social Theory and Values: A Hermeneutic Perspective. *Theory and Psychology,* **4**, 2, pp. 199–226.

Rifkin, J. (1989). *Entropy: Into the Greenhouse World.* New York: Bantam.

Rose, K. and J. Kincheloe (2003). *Art, Culture, and Education: Artful Teaching in a Fractured Landscape.* New York: Peter Lang.

Roth, W., K. Tobin and S. Ritchie (2001). *Re/constucting Elementary Science.* New York: Peter Lang.

Scering, G. (1997). Themes of a Critical/Feminist Pedagogy: Teacher Education for Democracy. *Journal of Teacher Education,* **48**, 1, pp. 62–69.

Schon, D. (1987). *Educating the Reflective Practitioner.* San Francisco: Jossey-Bass.

Schubert, W. (1998). Toward Constructivist Teacher Education for Elementary Schools in the Twenty-first Century: A Framework for Decision-Making. my.netian.com/~-yhhknue/coned19.htm

Sedgwick, E. (1995). Gosh, Boy George, You Must Be Awfully Secure in Your Masculinity! In M. Berger, B. Wallis and S. Watson (Eds.), *Constructing Masculinity.* New York: Routledge.

Segall, A. (2002). *Disturbing Practice: Reading Teacher Education as Text.* New York: Peter Lang.

Selfe, C. and R. Selfe (1994). The Politics of the Interface: Power and its Exercise in Electronic Contact Zones. http://www.hu.mtu.edu/~cyselfe/texts/politics.html

Semali, L. and J. Kincheloe (1999). *What Is Indigenous Knowledge? Voices from the Academy.* New York: Garland.

Shaker, P. and C. Kridel (1989). The Return to Experience: A Reconceptualist Call. *Journal of Teacher Education,* pp. 2–8.

Sherrard, C. (1991). Developing Discourse Analysis. *The Journal of General Psychology,* **118**, 2, pp. 171–79.

Simpson, D. and M. Jackson (2001). John Dewey and Educational Evaluation. In J. Kincheloe and D. Weil (Eds.) *Standards and Schooling in the U.S.: An Encyclopedia.*

Santa Barbara, CA: ABC-Clio.

Slaughter, R. (1989). Cultural Reconstruction in the Post-modern World. *Journal of Curriculum Studies, 3,* pp. 255–270.

Smith, D. (1999). *Pedagon: Interdisciplinary Essays in the Human Sciences, Pedagogy, and Culture.* New York: Peter Lang.

Snook, I. (1999). Teacher Education: Preparation for a Learned Profession. http://www.aare.edu.au/99pap/sno99148.htm

Soto, L. (Ed.) (2000). *The Politics of Early Childhood Education.* New York: Peter Lang.

Soto, L. (2001). Bilingual Education—Silenced Lives: The Case of Bilingual Children. In J. Kincheloe and D. Weil (Eds.), *Standards and Schooling in the United States: An Encyclopedia,* 3 vols. Santa Barbara, CA: ABC-Clio.

Steinberg, S. (2001). *Multi/intercultural Conversations: A Reader.* New York: Peter Lang.

Steinberg, S. (2004). Thinking Critically about Popular Culture. In D. Weil and J. Kincheloe (Eds.), *Critical Thinking and Learning: An Encyclopedia.* Westport, CT: Greenwood.

Steinberg, S. and J. Kincheloe (2004). *Kinderculture: The Corporate Construction of Childhood.* 2nd ed. Boulder, CO: Westview.

Steiner, S., M. Krank, P. McLaren and R. Bahruth (Eds.) (2000). *Freirean Pedagogy, Praxis, and Possibilities: Projects for the New Millennium.* New York: Garland.

Sumara, D. (1996). *Private Readings in Public: Schooling the Literary Imagination.* New York: Peter Lang.

Sumara, D. and B. Davis (1997). Cognition, Complexity, and Teacher Education. *Harvard Educational Review,* **67**, 1, pp. 75–104.

Suvin, D. (1988). Can People Be (Re) Presented in Fiction? Toward a Theory of Narrative Agents and a Materialist Critique beyond Technocracy or Reductionism. In C. Nelson and L. Grossberg (Eds.), *Marxism and the Interpretation of Culture.* Urbana: University of Illinois Press.

Taylor, P., B. Fraser and L. White (1994). CLES: An Instrument for Monitoring the Development of Constructivist Learning Environments. Paper Presented to the Annual Meeting of the American Educational Research Association, New Orleans. http://surveylearning.com/cles/papers/cles_aera94-award.htm

Teitelbaum, K. (2004). Curriculum Theorizing. In D. Weil and J. Kincheloe (Eds.) *Critical Thinking and Learning: An Encyclopedia*. Westport, CT: Greenwood.

Thayer-Bacon, B. (2000). *Transforming Critical Thinking: Thinking Constructively*. New York: Teachers College Press.

Thomas, G. (1998). The Myth of Rational Research. *British Educational Research Journal*, **24**,2.

Thompson, J. (1987). Language and Ideology: A Framework for Analysis. *The Sociological Review*. 35, pp. 516–36.

Thomson, C. (2001). Massification, Distance Learning and Quality in INSET Teacher Education: A Challenging Relationship. http://www.ru.ac.za/academic/adc/papers/Thomson.htm

Tobin, K. (1993). *The Practice of Constructivism in Science Education*. Washington, DC: AAAS Press.

Tobin, K. and Tippins, D. (1993). Constructivism as a Referent for Teaching and Learning. In K. Tobin (Ed.), *The Practice of Constructivism in Science Education*. pp. 3–31. Washington, DC: AAAS Press.

Van Hesteran, F. (1986). Counselling Research in a Different Key: The Promise of Human Science Perspective. *Canadian Journal of Counselling*, **20**, 4, pp. 200–34.

Varela, F. (1999). *Ethical Know-How: Action, Wisdom, and Cognition*. Stanford: Stanford University Press.

Vavrus, M. and O. Archibald (1998). Teacher Education Practices Supporting Social Justice: Approaching an Individual Self-Study Inquiry into Institutional Self-Study Process. Paper Presented to the Second International Conference on Self-Study of Teacher Education Practice, Herstmonceux Castle, UK.

von Glaserfeld, E. (1980). Adaptation and Viability. *American Psychologist*, 35, pp. 970–74.

von Glaserfeld, E. (1993). Questions and Answers about Radical Constructivism. In K. Tobin (Ed.) *Constructivism in Education*. Hillsdale, NJ: Lawrence Erlbaum.

Weil, D. and H. Anderson (Eds.), (2000). *Perspectives in Critical Thinking: Essays by Teachers in Theory and Practice*. New York: Peter Lang.

Welch, S. (1985). *Communities of Resistance and Solidarity*. Maryknoll, NY: Orbis.

Wertsch, J. (1991). *Voices of the Mind: A Sociocultural Approach to Mediated Action*. Cambridge, MA: Harvard University Press.

Wertsch, J. and P. Tulviste (1992). L.S. Vygotsky and Contemporary Developmental Psychology. *Developmental*

Psychology, **28**, 4, pp. 548–57.

Wexler, P. (2000). *The Mystical Society: Revitalization in Culture, Theory, and Education*. Boulder, CO: Westview.

Williams, S. (1999). Truth, Speech, and Ethics: A Feminist Revision of Free Speech Theory. *Genders*, 30. http://www.genders.org

Willinsky, J. (2001a). Raising the Standards for Democratic Education: Research and Evaluation as Public Knowledge. In J. Kincheloe and D. Weil (Eds.) *Standards and Schooling in the U.S.: An Encyclopedia*. Santa Barbara, CA: ABC-Clio.

Willinsky, J. (2001b). *After Literacy: Essays*. New York: Peter Lang.

Wirth, A. (1983). *Productive Work—In Industry and Schools*. Lanham, MD: University Press of America.

Yeakey, C. (1987). Critical Thought and Administrative Theory: Conceptual Approaches to the Study of Decision-Making. *Planning and Changing*, **18**, 1, pp. 23–32.

Young, I. (1992). Five Faces of Oppression. In T. Wartenberg (Ed.), *Rethinking Power*. Albany: State University of New York Press.

Young, M. (1971). *Knowledge and Control: New Directions for the Sociology of Education*, London: Macmillan.

Young, T. and J. Yarbrough (1993). *Reinventing Sociology: Mission and Methods for Postmodern Sociologists*. Red Feather Institute. Transforming Sociology Series, 154.

Zammito, J. (1996). Historicism, Metahistory, and Historical Practice: The Historicization of the Historical Subject. http://home.cc.umanitoba.ca/~sprague/zammito.htm

Zappulla, C. (1997). *Suffering in Silence: Teachers with AIDS and the Moral School Community*. New York: Peter Lang.

Zavarzadeh, M. and D. Morton (1991). *Theory, (Post)modernity, Opposition*. Washington, DC: Maison-neuve.

Zeno, G. (1998). A Cultural Critique of the Use of Networked Electronic Discourse in a Liberatory Composition Pedagogy. http://ocbbs.odessa.edu/public/oc/staff_dept/mjorday/index.htm.

Zuss, M. (1999). *Subject Present: Life-Writings and Strategies of Representation*. New York: Peter Lang.